HOW TO BUILD THE
ULTIMATE V-TWIN
MOTORCYCLE

by Timothy Remus

D1306598

Published by:
Wolfgang Inc.
13895 - 236th St.
Scandia, MN 55073

First published in 1995 by Wolfgang Publications Inc., 13895 236th St. No. Scandia, MN 55073, USA.

The information in this book is true and complete to the best of our knowledge. All recommendations are made without any guarantee on the part of the author or publisher, who also disclaim any liability incurred in connection with the use of this data or specific details.

We recognize that some words, model names and designations, for example, mentioned herein are the property of the trademark holder. We use them for identification purposes only. This is not an official publication.

ISBN number: 0-9641358-2-5

Printed and bound in the USA

On the Cover:

The soft-tail style bike with the electric blue paint job is the creation of Mike McAllister from M-C specialties, Blaine, Minnesota.

How To Build
The Ultimate V-Twin Motorcycle
Contents

Acknowledgements

During the years that I worked as a mechanic, I never much liked having someone hang over my shoulder, watching every move I made. So I am extra grateful to the motorcycle mechanics and fabricators who allowed me to do just that - and take photos to boot.

The list includes Richard Rohda from Minneapolis Custom, Mike McAllister from M-C Specialties and Elmer, Lee and Bug from Kokesh Motorcycle Accessories. Donnie Smith and Rob Roehl must be used to me by now - in fact I spend so much time in Donnie's shop I keep thinking maybe I'm an employee.

I also need to thank George Edwards at St. Paul Harley-Davidson for his help, the rest of the crew at Kokesh MC, and Steve Laugtug for pushing his project along so I could take photos.

These projects all take longer than they're supposed to and there were days when I really wondered if this particular book would ever get done. Without Mike Urseth and Amy Huberty to do the layout it never would have been completed.

For proof reading I have to thank Jason Mitchell and also my lovely and talented wife, Mary Lanz.

Introduction

Yes, you can build your own motorcycle

Why build a bike from scratch? There are at least three good reasons, beginning with the long wait and speculation that surrounds the purchase of many new bikes. Reason number two is the high cost and waste of buying a perfectly good motorcycle and then ripping it apart to make it better. Third is the fact that by beginning with nothing more than a series of catalogs you can build exactly the motorcycle you want with only minimal compromises.

Is a soft-tail bike better than a rubber-mount, how much rake is too much and do I really need a 96 cubic inch engine? This book is meant to help you answer those questions and assemble that pile of parts into a running bike.

For all the great information contained in this book there are a few things it is not. This is not a service or parts manual. You will encounter many questions during the assembly of your new bike that are not answered here. For example, the correct torque specification for the clutch hub nut is not contained in these pages. The answer to that question is contained in a good service manual and I recommend you go out and buy one. Experienced builders also suggest you buy a parts manual at the same time.

When it comes time to buy the parts for your new ride, consider buying the bulk of those parts from one store. Pick the store carefully, not for the best price but for the quality of personnel. No matter how many books you buy, questions will arise that you can't answer. That's when it's nice if you know the guy who assembles bikes all day long, or the counter person who sells parts just like yours.

By making the bulk of your purchases from one store, you build a report with the sales and service people there. Now you can legitimately ask questions as to which is the right inner primary or whether or not to use sealer on a particular gasket. No one likes to look dumb, but sometimes you can save a tremendous amount of time and hassle by admitting your ignorance and simply asking for help.

Consider too that there will be some parts of the project you may not be qualified to do. Engine assembly, wiring and paint are three that come to mind. If the shop that sells you the parts does at least some of the assembly, they have an added stake in selling you the best parts.

Your by-word for this project should be quality: Quality parts from a quality motorcycle shop. Quality assembly that comes when you take your time, or ask good people to take their time. This is not going to be a cheap project. So spend a few extra bucks to ensure everything is done right. The result will be a quality motorcycle that you built yourself.

Chapter One

Decide What To Build

The hardest part of the whole job.

Building your own motorcycle from the ground up is a tall order. One of the toughest parts of that job is the planning and decision making that come *before* you buy any parts or turn any wrenches. In some ways it's easier to buy your new ride from the dealer. At least that way you only get so many choices. A limited number of chassis are available, all equipped with the same basic engine (with fuel injection available on some models). Sure there are options in terms of paint and accessories, but the total number of decisions you have

Owned by the infamous Jose' and built at Anderson Studios in Nashville, this Kenny Boyce framed hot rod is a good example of what you can do by combining mechanical ability with creative talent.

to make is limited.

A bike built from scratch on the other hand is kind of overwhelming simply because there are so many possibilities. You are no longer limited by the catalog from Milwaukee. While chassis selection still falls into two categories, the twin-shock or soft-tail style, the number of each type available from all the manufacturers is large and growing. And many manufacturers allow you to modify the rake and stretch, and add a pro-street kit if you need that fat 180 series tire in the back.

Once you decide on the frame style and dimensions the next big choice is the engine. How many cubes do you want, fed by which carburetor, breathing into which set of heads? What's the best way to ensure that the carb you choose will work correctly with the camshaft, heads and exhaust? More decisions, and each one as important as the one before.

DESIGNING THE NEW BIKE

You aren't just building a machine, you're designing a complete motorcycle. Start with a budget figure. Be realistic about what it will cost and how much you have to spend. Avoid the trap of over-optimism because it leads to bikes that don't get finished or don't get finished on time.

Next determine how the bike will be used. Big stroker motors sound great and make gobs of torque but don't have the longevity of a mildly souped-up 80 cubic inch V-Twin.

Last but not least, determine the style for the new bike. Which frame, equipped with which fenders and tank(s) will provide the look you're after. What color will the new bike be and who will do the final paint

The Style Glide from Nempco is built from their catalog parts, including a soft-tail style chassis and tanks stretched with their new kit. Nempco

Pro Street Sweeper is from Sumax, based on their Pro Comp frame with Street Sweeper fenders and air cleaner manufactured from composite fiberglass. Sumax

7

work. There is a tendency to skimp on the paint job and spend that "extra" money on hardware. Before you decide to be penny wise and pound foolish consider that the paint is the one thing that people immediately see when they view your bike. It's the biggest, most visible part of your new design. They might not notice the button head bolts or the billet engine cases, but everyone will notice the paint job. As professional bike builder Donnie Smith is fond of saying, "It's the paint that really makes the bike."

MONEY, MONEY, MONEY

The one limitation we all share is money. So your first decision is simply a realistic look at how much money you're going to spend (for help with financing see Chapter 6). Of that money, you need to decide how much will be spent on outside labor. Stated another way, how much of the building are you going to turn over to someone else.

What you really need here is a budget. Not a rough calculation done on the napkin at the bar but an honest to god list of each major part and its cost. Then another series of line items is necessary, one for each outside labor operation - paint, powder coating, possible upholstery. Enter each item and its cost. Be realistic on the cost. Don't assume your old buddy from the Army will mold and paint the frame for fifty bucks and a twelve pack. Don't forget the "miscellaneous" category for all the little things that don't have categories of their own. Things like the chrome Allen bolts you want to use throughout the bike and the billet mirrors from the Arlen Ness or Pro One catalog.

After you've answered the first question, "How much money can I spend," there's one more very important question you have to ask yourself. "How do I ride, how will I use this motorcycle?"

USAGE

If this is going to be your only bike and you want to ride it to Sturgis then you probably don't want a big stroker motor in a soft-tail style chassis (unless you're *really* tough). For riders who cover lots of miles a rubber-mount twin-shock frame that isn't slammed to the ground would probably be a better choice. If, on the

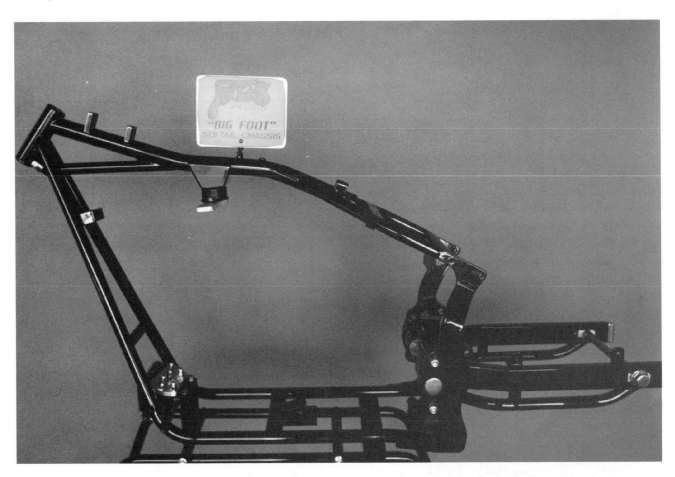

Most soft-tail style chassis mount the motor direct to the frame. This Big Foot soft-tail style chassis from Atlas, however uses a rubber-mounted engine and transmission - and will accept a 190 series rear tire with belt drive. Atlas

other hand, you already own a nice Dresser and the new bike is intended to be the proverbial bar-hopper you probably want a very hot motor and an even hotter paint job.

A MATTER OF STYLE

After you've been brutally honest with yourself about how you're going to use the bike and how much money you can spend you need to consider style. What exactly do you want this machine to look like? Is nostalgia your goal, or something more new-wave with bright neon graphics.

Professional bike builders send potential customers home with a stack of magazines and orders to, "mark all the bikes you really like." You may also have your own photo-file of favorite bikes. You might even want to build a bike very close to one of the new models from Milwaukee. Whatever the case, you need a picture or detailed sketch of what the new bike will look like. Unless you've built bikes before it's dangerous to just "let it happen." The plans and sketches should be detailed - you don't need a fifteen thousand dollar surprise.

Experienced builders often start with a photo of a bike similar to the one they want to build. At the local copy and printing store they make big black and white blow-ups of the photo. Now they can "customize" the bike with scissors and glue. A different fork rake is just a matter of cut and paste. A new color can be had simply by purchasing some colored markers. Cut, paste and then make more copies. This is a cheap way to visualize and finalize your plans for the new bike.

If your plans run to the more exotic, you can hire an artist to do a color rendering of the new bike, based on your ideas as seen through the artist's eye. Arlen Ness often starts with a

With the right kit you can convert your wide-glide to a Heritage style fork assembly Custom Chrome.

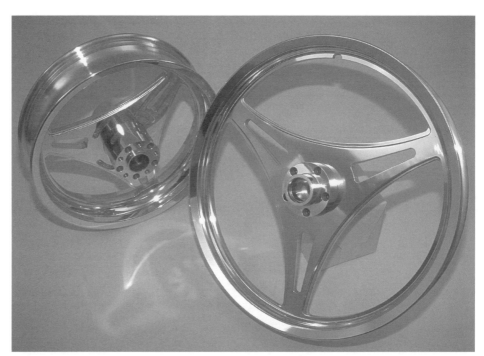

The wheels are a major part of any motorcycle design, so chose yours with care. Among the new designs are these three spoke wheels from Nempco.

Built in-house this "convertible" features the new Arlen Ness fairing and saddle bags, along with tail-dragger fenders and a stretched aluminum gas tank.

photo of the rolling chassis and then lays tracing paper over the photo. This way any sketches of the new body panels or gas tank are superimposed on the rolling chassis - so they're sure to fit the actual dimensions of the bike.

COMPROMISE

Money, style and the intended use are the three things that will determine the type of bike you build. Seldom do all three categories agree. Even if you have enough money to build the bike you really want (an unlikely event for most of us) you may find that a soft-tail frame gives the right "look" but falls short in the long-haul ride-ability department.

The process is much like building a new house. Once you've settled on the total dollars it's often a matter of trade-offs. A bigger kitchen is nice but it means stealing space from the living room. Elaborate bathrooms are all the rage, but the extra space (and money) has to come from within the total overall budget.

When conflicts arise, and they will, you need to decide which parts of your new design are the most important. The new billet wheels are great, but for the price of two wheels you can pay for the paint job, or sheet metal or pair of aftermarket cylinder heads. Work through the give and take until you've designed a bike you can enjoy and be proud to call your own - one that can be built within your budget.

TIME IS LIKE DIA-MONDS

As you assemble the plan and budget for the new bike

This mock-up of a Steve Laugtug bike shows a late model rubber-mount drive train in an Arlen Ness frame. FLT transmissions like this one mount the oil tank underneath and thus open up the area under the seat.

consider the time factor as well. Especially if you've never built a bike before, this is going to take more than a week. Because of the mock-up stage (more later) you will essentially build the bike twice. There's nothing more frustrating than having the parts in the garage and no time to assemble them into a running bike. Frustration leads to haste and haste opens the door to sloppy work.

You need a plan made up of realistic costs and realistic goals. Try to set aside enough time to do the job and do it right. Set a schedule that's flexible but keeps you plugging along toward the end goal. Stay organized with a list of "things to do" and "parts I need." When the job of building a bike gets overwhelming, break it down into smaller jobs like assembling the fork or installing the motor. Avoid the temptation to change the style of the bike half way through the project. Stick with your original design and work it through to completion. You need a good plan to start with, because if you start second guessing the design half way through the project you'll never get finished.

The rewards are great - a new motorcycle of your own manufacture. One with the equipment and paint that *you* want. But it ain't easy and it ain't cheap. So

plan carefully. Be sure you've got enough money (or almost enough) and time to do it the right way the first time.

INTERVIEW:
ROB CARLSON FROM
KOKESH MOTORCYCLE ACCESSORIES

Rob Carlson is part owner of Kokesh Motorcycle Accessories, a well-known Minneapolis shop, and builders of the soft-tail style custom seen in Chapter Seven.

Kokesh is what you might call a full-service motorcycle shop with a full parts counter and showroom, as well as a shop with three mechanics. Over the years a lot of bikes have been built and modified in the Kokesh shop - which gives Rob a unique perspective on this whole business of building bikes from scratch.

The interview with Rob concerns the hardest parts of the building process - how to decide exactly what to build, and how to build it for a reasonable amount of cash.

Rob, if I'm a new buyer who comes into your shop

This sleek soft-tail bike carries the new Street Sweeper fenders designed by Paul Erpenbeck.

These high quality Nitralloy cases from Sputhe make a great foundation for a high performance engine. Arlen Ness Inc.

Rubber-mount chassis often use a FXR-style transmission like this one. The pivot shaft for the swingarm passes through the boss at the rear of the case.

and wants to build a bike, how do you get me pointed in the right direction, there are so many choices to make?

I hope that when you come in you already have some kind of preconceived idea of what you want to do or some conception of the bike you want to have done. I think it's really hard trying to steer a guy one way or another. Most people want to build a bike that looks like a friend's bike or one they saw in a magazine.

What if I'm a little farther along with my ideas for a whole bike when I come in the store, how do you work with me to make sure my ideas make sense?

We start with a general idea of what kind of bike it's going to be. Whether it's going to be a stock soft-tail style bike that we customize just a little bit, or a more radical soft-tail, FXR, or Dresser. We get some general sense of what you want to do and then we start elaborating on each individual component on the bike. Say you want to do an Atlas-framed bike like the one we did for Henry Thomas (professional football player). Once we know which frame, then we can start with what kind of wheels you like and the look you're trying to achieve. You need to decide on the fenders and tanks. Once we've got the general idea of what the bike is going to look like, then we can go into the separate components like the motor - how big do you want the motor, what kind of riding are we going to do. Money is also a factor - we have to discuss how much money you really have to spend.

As long as we're talking about money, what's the bottom line to build a bike from scratch?

This Low Glide soft-tail style frame from Custom Chrome is available in OEM style for a simple and less expensive bike, or as a "custom" frame with more rake and a wider rear section for a wide tire look.

From Sturgis Wheel Company, these bright wheels offer the looks of a billet wheel in a less expensive cast design. Mid-USA.

If a guy has a little bit of mechanical ability and can put most of it together himself, I think realistically, especially with new components and stuff, they start at about thirteen to fourteen thousand dollars, it goes up from there. Really, the sky's the limit.

If we decide that what I need is a soft-tail bike because it's got the look that I want, how do I pick a soft-tail style frame?

It depends on what components you want to use around it. Not so much the drive train, but the front end, the sheet metal, and what kind of wheels you want to go with. Say you just want to go with the stock wheels, I would just try to steer you to a more inexpensive stock style replacement frame. Whether it be a Tripoli or Santee, whatever it might be. Now if you want something a little more elaborate, fat tires, things molded in, some unusual front-end configuration or something, then you might want to go with an Atlas or half a dozen other manufacturers out there.

Are most of the frames good quality, or do I have to be careful what I buy?

There are brands you have to watch out for. I hate to bring up names... You have to ask around, ask people who build bikes or sell a lot of frames, they know which are the best brands. I've had some frames where the gas tank mounts weren't right and the motor mounts were way off - so you can't line the inner primary up with the transmission. We always take care of it but it's a time consuming process. I like to use brands I've used before that I know are good.

The soft-tail style frames, those are mostly set up for fat-bob type tanks?

You can get most of those with or without the mounts if you just request the frame that way. Almost all the companies will have what they call a "build sheet." You'll have to tell them what rake and stretch you want, and possibly a wide rear section if that's an option.

You can easily build that engine for show as well as go - with billet beauties like the rocker covers, lifter blocks and cam cover from Arlen Ness.

In terms of dimensions, stretch and rake, if I'm unsure how far to go, what is your advice?

We can show you pictures of different bikes, what a certain rake may look like or what you can achieve with it. If you want a nice short, stubby bike of course, you probably want a stock rake. If you want a long, lean bike, then you might want to go three degrees over. And maybe you want to add some stretch to the frame to really lock in that longer look. But remember, a stretched frame will need stretched tanks or custom sheet metal.

When does extra rake become too much rake, when does the handling start to get strange or heavy in town? At what point do you start to make a lot of trade-offs?

Anything over five extra degrees (additional) starts getting too radical for me. Although there are people like Donnie Smith and some other builders who go beyond that a lot of times. I guess it depends on whatever that person feels comfortable with, but I don't like it any more than five degrees, so that's probably about 37 degrees total.

The wide tire look is popular now, do most of the frame manufacturers offer a wide-drive kit as an option?

Yes, Tripoli, Atlas and Pro One all do. There's probably a half dozen different ones to chose from. One thing to keep in mind, once you decide to run a big fat rear tire everything starts going up in price. Everything won't bolt on like it will on a stock bike. Now you have to work harder to line up the rear wheel so the price starts going up dramatically.

If people mount a one-piece gas tank and there

aren't any pre-fabricated mounts, typically, how do you guys mount those?

Well, we weld brand new mounts on. That's what you have to do, make your own mounts. Typically on the bottom of the tank so they're out of sight.

When it comes to mounting gas tanks the fat-bob

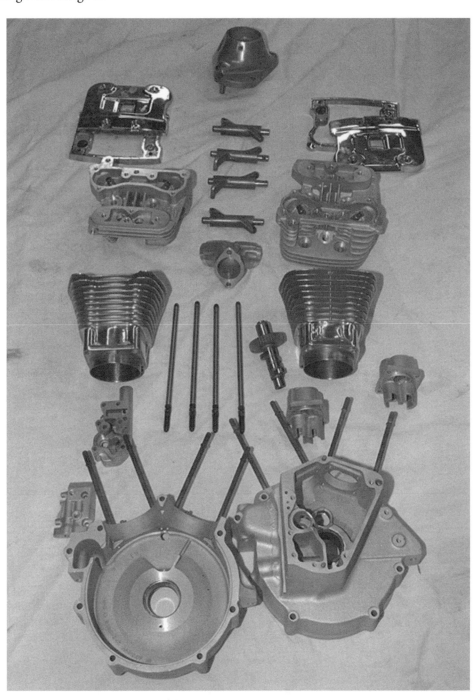

When it comes time to put an engine in the frame, you can either buy all the parts and have it assembled, or purchase a complete assembled motor.

style tanks come in both solid and rubber-mounted (sometimes called "flat sided") styles. Do you have a preference?

Well, on all of the older Harley-Davidsons the tanks were bolted solid to the frame and they worked just fine. I think if everything is constructed correctly it's OK to use solid mounts. I don't think it has to have a rubber mount. But the new tanks are rubber mounted, they're good tanks and they don't break. With the FXR bikes (sometimes called rubber-mounts) the engine is so isolated with the rubber mounts that there is no problem with mounting those tanks solid to the frame - that's the way the factory does it.

All these soft-tail style frames mount the engine solid to the frame?

Almost all of them. Atlas has one they call their Bigfoot, it's a rubber mount. It uses the FXR or FLT drivetrain. And Tripoli makes one also.

Now I have the frame, how do you help me decide which, and how much, motor to buy?

I guess we figure out what kind of riding you want to do. Whether it's mostly cruising for example. In which case I'd just suggest building a stock mill, with just a little bit of head work for example. Maybe even a stock ignition just to make the reliability better.

It really comes back to the riding you want to do. Because a motor, up to a certain point, is not going to cost you that much more if you want to add some power. If you want more power or a bigger motor we can show you several different mills or sizes and see what you feel comfortable with. We might try to talk you out of the real wild ones because the reliability starts going down.

Is it cheaper, if you're on the bottom edge of the budget, to buy a crate motor from Harley or put something together from pieces?

It's probably a little bit cheaper to go with the crate motor and get a matching transmission. The carburetor and alternator are already on there, you're set to go. It's pretty hard to build a motor and tranny for that same price.

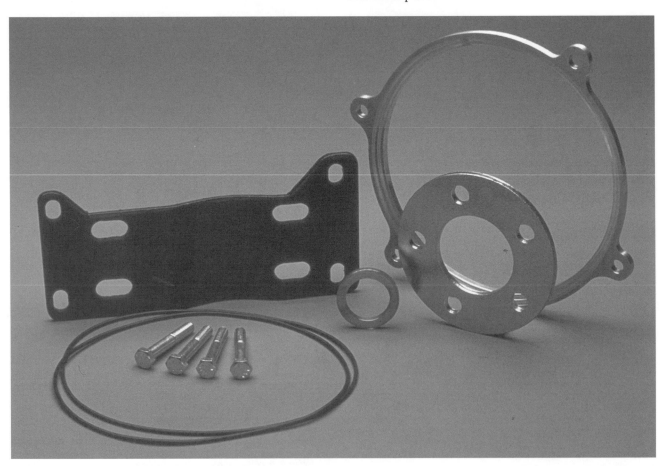

A wider rear tire can be adapted to many soft-tail style chassis with this kit from Arlen Ness that moves the transmission over to the left. Arlen Ness Inc.

What about the longevity of a high-horsepower motor?

I think the problem with speed and go-fast motors is that the more power that's there, the more you're going to use it and get on it. That's a big part of what cuts down the motor life.

If I want more horse power in this new engine, what are some common "packages" you might suggest? I realize there are a million possibilities.

If a guy's going to go with a Harley-Davidson motor and just wants it to be just little bit faster, maybe we would just port the existing heads, shave them for more compression,

As you plan out that new machine, don't overlook the little things. Polished and chrome bolt kits are available to replace those unsightly cadmium plated bolts. Drag Specialties.

These engine cases from Delkron are available in late and early style (for generator models back to '55) and also in a big-bore model. Drag Specialties.

add a different cam and work with the stock carburetor. The Keihin CV (constant velocity) carb is actually a pretty good carburetor. Or you can add an S&S or maybe a Mikuni carburetor.

If you want a little bit more then that, then you probably want to buy a complete motor instead of building one. Because by the time you disassemble the motor and modify the cases for a stroker crank or a big-bore kit it isn't cost effective. You're better off getting one of the S&S motors, they've come out with a lot of neat stuff lately. Even if you're on a budget S&S is making some interesting motors. If a guy's on a tight budget, say he's already got an early-style Shovelhead frame and most of the components, even a four-speed transmission, he could put an evolution motor in the frame and get the reliability and horsepower out of it.

I'm talking about two of the S&S motors, one is a 79 inch and one is an 84 cubic inch. Brand new. They fit right into the stock frames and the price is very reasonable. There are some things that S&S doesn't make (Editor's note: this is changing as we speak). The rocker box covers, and rocker arms assemblies, push rod covers, cam cover - that's about it - you have to supply those parts. Otherwise everything is supplied including the carburetor.

Then from there, the sky's the limit?

Yeah. It really is. For the guys that want a little bit more power, but still want a dependable, street-able bike that really hits hard when they twist the throttle, I guess we've been steering them mostly to the 96 inch motor that S&S supplies. They have what they call a "hot set up" and it's a deal that you can buy as a kit or assembled. This motor is about two to three hundred dollars cheaper than any other motors they have. That's probably the most popular motor they're making right now, the 96 inch. You can buy it as a long block or a short block. Again the long block would still require the rocker boxes, rocker arms and cam cover.

In terms of power I think you're looking at right around 100 horsepower right out of the crate, so that's pretty good. I think a Harley-Davidson engine is about 60 horsepower.

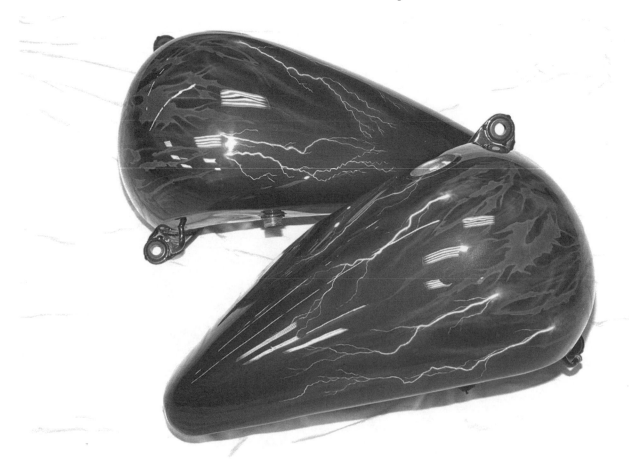

Don't make the mistake of spending fifteen thousand on the bike and only a few hundred on the paint job. Painted by Jerry Snyder, these rubber-mount factory fat-bob tanks are intended for the bike seen in Chapter 8.

For a guy at home who maybe didn't want to pay you to assemble the motor, he can just buy that as a unit?

Right, but one thing to keep in mind if you do get it assembled, they are not painted. It depends on what you want to achieve for final looks, but sometimes the unpainted motor and transmission looks a little bit plain. And it's easier to do a nice job of painting the motor when it's disassembled.

You said earlier that it's relatively easy to get horsepower up to about 100, but that beyond that it comes more dearly?

When you order wheels, be specific as to the frame and swingarm. That way you're more likely to get the right wheel and hub for your bike. Arlen Ness Inc.

Yes. Once you get past 100 horsepower you have to start doing some major and financially challenging things to get the extra horsepower out of it. Whether it be a big stroker or big bore and/or head work too. You have to put real expensive components in there and the reliability starts going way down. It's pretty hard to get past 100 horses and be reliable and cheap. To get up to 130 or 140 horsepower some of those guys have a starting point of ten or eleven thousand bucks, up to thirty thousand dollars for just the motor.

What are some of the mistakes that riders make when they build a motor or have one built?

A big one is camshafts. People always think the higher the lift the more power it will make, but it's not always true. Most of us drive in the lower rpm range, 2,000 to 5,000, and that's where you want the power. People are putting cams in there that don't even turn-on until 4,500 or 5,000 rpm so they're "over camming" them.

Is that the biggest mistake they make?

Aluminum wheels come in cast and "billet" designs. While these are cast from 356 aluminum the billet wheels are generally cut from 6061 aluminum. Billet wheels tend to be lighter - and more expensive.

I think so. Everyone always thinks bigger is better. No matter what it is, and with cams it really doesn't work that way. If you have a cruiser motor, even if it's a big bore and stroke, I think a good rule of thumb is to pick less cam than what you think you want. You'll end up with more power and it will be in available in the RPM range where you ride.

What are the other mistakes they make when they try to get more horsepower out of the motor and try to go faster?

The cam is the biggest mistake. Another one is big carburetors. Just because it's bigger they think it's going to work better. Some of them put a S&S G series carb on an 80 cubic inch motor. Or they'll combine parts that don't generally work well together. Whether it be the pipes working with the cam, or the carburetor or the headwork, all those parts have to work together to get good power.

Before they go buy the cam and pipes they should talk to a good motor man or sit down with a computer program (see the Engine chapter for more on the pro-gram Rob is referring to). They should really do their homework before they start buying parts.

We have to put a transmission behind this motor, what do we have for options? Is the factory unit the best value again?

Yes it is, by far. You can get a Harley-Davidson transmission complete for less than fifteen hundred dollars (prices may vary from dealer to dealer) and it's hard to build one for that. Some guys put in the Andrews gears, but the only advantage is the fact that they're back cut so they do shift a little bit better. Harley-Davidson has a new gear set known as HCR (high contact ratio) gears. It's like a constant mesh gear. They're full contact gears installed in 1995, and later, transmissions. These are nice and they're noticeably quieter than all the other gear sets out there.

There are not really a lot of choices for transmissions. You can go to a Delkron case if you want or a factory case. But for gears, the only aftermarket gears are from Andrews and RevTech. And as long as you're not racing the Harley-Davidson transmission will stand

Not your typical scratch-built bike, this long flowing design was conceived by Arlen Ness and designed by Carl Brouhad. Hand formed panels are the work of master tin-man Craig Naff.

up just fine, even if you put one of those bigger S&S engines in the frame.

In terms of clutches and the rest of the drive train, is there a point at which you need something better than stock?

I think so. Especially if you have an older clutch set up, prior to 1990. Those ones did slip. They were pretty notorious. The factory changed them in 1990, and the newer ones are a lot better, but there are still better ones out there. I guess the nicest one, from our experience anyway, is the Bandit clutch. It's a really nice unit. It's very soft to the feel and it's either engaged or disengaged. Otherwise, I have been using stock clutch hubs with the Barnett Kevlar clutch plates for the guy who wants to use more of the stock components. They work pretty well too. And neither of these clutch options are very expensive.

*Rob Carlson of
Kokesh MC Accessories*

How about the front end. How do you feel about front ends, and what do you like and not like?

I like to stay as close to an OEM front end as possible. The Ceriani front ends are quite expensive for what you get. If you're building a soft-tail style bike I'd rather steer you toward a standard wide-glide fork assembly. Any of the newer wide glides are 41 mm tubes, they have good fork action and good steering characteristics. I think any of them would be a good choice whether you want to go to Heritage or Softail Custom style.

I really don't care for the Springer too much. I don't like the handling characteristics and I don't care for 21 inch front tires like they have on the Softail Custom. Obviously some people like that, but it still won't handle like a 16 or 19 inch tire and wheel. On the FXR or twin-shock frames I'm more apt to just put a 39 mm narrow glide fork assembly on and be done.

The factory set ups are nice. You can clean them off, chrome, or polish them. You can make them look real nice and I think they're the best value out there for the money.

How about if we close by asking you what kind of mistakes people make. Not just with engine equipment, but when they go into a deal like this, where do they get in trouble and where do they screw up?

Most people run over budget, that's the biggest mistake everyone makes. I try to warn them right from the beginning, "This is going to cost you fifteen thousand dollars," but they still think in their head they can do it for ten thousand. Pretty soon their project, instead of being a 6 or 8 month project, is a two or three year project with no end in sight.

I think almost any good parts guy who's been doing it for awhile will probably tell you how much it's going to cost within ten or fifteen percent. Another thing I don't like that people do, and I guess it's a personal thing, I hate to see a guy who just spent thirteen or fourteen thousand bucks on a bike get a five hundred dollar paint job.

Advice for brakes and wheels?

I guess wheels and brakes are pretty self explanatory. That's a personal thing really. What do you like and what does it cost. Some of the wheels are very ridiculous in price, same with the brakes. The Harley brakes are probably the cheapest ones out there and they work great. Some riders want a little bit more braking power and they put the nice Performance Machine calipers and rotors on- but the cost starts going way up. And there are a bunch of new ones out. RevTech and Arlen Ness have both brought out new calipers and there's a new Wilwood caliper, those are all good quality components. It's really a matter of taste more than anything else.

Any more words of wisdom?

Well some of the components on the market today are maybe a little overkill, like the 6 piston calipers. Most of it is probably show, so the rider can go down to Whiskey Junction (the local two-wheeled watering hole) and talk about it. But it is nice to see people putting on high quality suspension and brake components.

I think most of the choppers today are actually road worthy - finally! I'm sure you remember what they were like in the 70's and early 80's. I rode the same things. Ten-inch-over tubes, no front brakes, little or no rear brake. Damned dangerous. I guess most things that people are doing right now actually do work. These are bikes you can ride. So maybe something good has come about in the evolution of things.

Chapter Two

The Frame

Like The Foundation Under Your House.

As you plan out the new bike your choice of a frame is one of the most important decisions you will make. Though it's a pretty obvious statement, your choice of a frame will have a major impact on the way your bike looks and handles. You really need to know how you're going to use the bike and what kinds of compromises you're willing to make before you put down that hard-earned cash for the skeleton and foundation of your new machine.

If you're new to the ranks of V-Twin ownership

Built by Dave Perewitz, this Softail has a look that would be hard to match with a twin-shock frame.

ask experienced riders about the advantages and disadvantages of the various frame designs. Don't forget that for everything you gain there is also something you give up. The hard-tail look and great lines of a soft-tail style chassis are off-set by the limited suspension travel and the solid mounted (in most cases) engine. A fork that hangs out at forty or more degrees might give your bike a really bitchin' profile but it will also give it heavy handed manners at slow speed and a turn circle bigger than that needed by a Mack truck.

Building a bike is more than just bolting together a

The rake of the front fork will have a major impact on the both the way the bike looks and handles.

They don't have to be long and stretched to be good looking. Built at Departure Bike Works in Richmond Virginia, this short business-like Kenny Boyce framed bike looks good without the standard extended frame and forty degree rake.

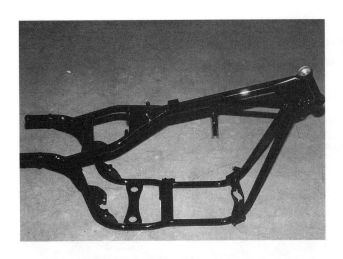

There are a number of twin-shock, rubber mount frames on the market - this Pro Comp frame from Sumax comes ready for fat-bob tanks and features 2 inches of stretch and a 35 degree fork angle.

Among the more popular after-market twin-shock frames are the offerings from Kenny Boyce. These frames are welded up from .095 inch thick tubing and come with gas tank mounts already in place or in "raw" form.

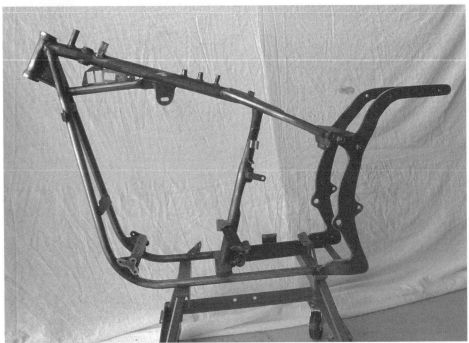

In the raw - this is the Tripoli frame, before powder coating, that will be assembled into the soft-tail bike seen in Chapter 8.

series of components. This is an exercise in design, not an abstract one but a design you're going to ride and ride and ride. You need to know what you want and what you're willing to give up to get it - because you're going to have to live with those decisions for a long time.

FRAMING THE DECISION

Frames come in three basic styles with a large number of variations. As stated earlier, your basic consideration are hard-tail, soft-tail (with the shocks hidden under the chassis) or a twin-shock frame (sometimes called FXR type).

Before discussing your frame options we need to get a few terms out of the way first. Rake is the angle of the fork assembly when compared to vertical. Some builders talk about a frame being "raked five degrees." What they mean is that it has five additional degrees of rake. A frame that is "stretched two inches" has extra material in the top tube. It is two inches longer - between the seat and the neck - than it was originally (or than a similar factory frame).

HARD-TAIL

A hard-tail frame makes a nice basis for a strictly-business kind of hot rod machine. By eliminating the rear suspension the frame is made simpler and less expensive. Hard-tail frames have those great lines, the look of a classic V-Twin. The down side is

A demonstration using two older Donnie Smith built FXRs. The bike in the foreground has an additional five degrees of rake, which gives it "an attitude."

ers think a soft-tail frame is the only one to have and the only way to build a bike that truly has "the look." Bikes that feature elaborate body work are often based on soft-tail frames because by eliminating the shocks from their traditional location it is much easier to wrap body work around the rear wheel and the area under the seat.

Yet there is always a cost, and for all the styling advantages of a soft-tail style frame there is a penalty. First, the soft-tail type design allows for only about three inches

the proverbial pounding your backside will take on any extended rides.

Though you might think a hard-tail is a hard-tail, there are a number of interesting alternatives for builders seeking these simplest of frame designs. In addition to rake angles, you can buy your hard-tail frame "stretched" (made longer between the seat and the neck) or with stretched lower legs which raises the neck and provides a much different look.

Some hardtails come with a "wishbone" shape in the front downtubes, and some provide for rubber-mounted engines. Most of the modern hard-tails will accept any Big Twin engine though many are designed for the four-speed transmission. New designs with wider rear sections allow the use of fat rear tires and belt drive.

Soft-tail

By hiding the shocks under the frame a soft-tail style frame provides the look of a hardtail without the harsh ride. Some clever builders have combined a soft-tail frame with an early-style springer front end and a seat that hides the pivot for a pretty convincing imitation of a true hard-tail.

The soft-tail frame can be the basis for some very good looking custom bikes, with lines and simplicity un-matched by twin-shock frames. Some rid-

Here you can see exactly how a typical FXR frame is raked. The neck area is cut most of the way through, then stretched back to the desired angle, set up in a jig so everything stays straight, and finally heli-arc welded back together.

A classic in it's own right, this Arlen Ness rubber-mount five-speed frame has been the basis of many a fine custom motorcycle.

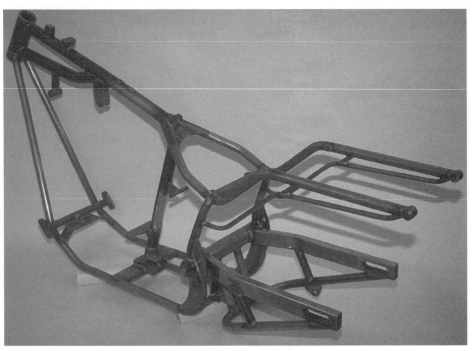

From Nempco comes this somewhat unusual soft-tail frame design with interesting tubular fender struts. Nempco

of suspension travel, meaning the ride will never match that of twin-shock bikes with about five inches of travel (this situation gets even worse if you lower the bike, further reducing the suspension travel). Second, most soft-tail type frames mount the engine solid to the frame meaning the full vibratory ability of that V-Twin will be fed to the frame and, ultimately, you the rider. Third, though somewhat subjective in nature, many riders who have ridden both styles of bikes feel a twin-shock frame handles and rides better than the soft-tail design.

Most soft-tail style frames will accept any Big Twin engine equipped with either a four or five speed transmission. Some of the newer designs are just a little taller than the factory frames, meaning they will accept a stroker engine with ease. Many of these frames can be ordered with a wider swingarm and provisions for a wide rear tire and belt drive.

TWIN-SHOCK

Twin-shock frames have been manufactured since the dawn of suspended time. This is a tried and true design providing plenty of suspension travel and (generally) good road manners. The twin-shock frame makes it easy to adjust the ride height up or down by installing longer or shorter shock absorbers. And though most soft-tail frames mount the motor to the frame in a solid fashion, most twin-shock frames are "rubber-mounted." By suspending the engine and transmission in rubber the vibes of the big thumping V-Twin are isolated from the rider for a smother ride and minimized fatigue after a long ride.

The disadvantages of this design include the look, which some riders just don't care for, and the fact that the shocks make it tough to wrap custom sheet metal around the back of the bike.

Though for many years there were only a few of these designs to chose from, like the Arlen Ness rubber-mount five-speed frame and some OEM (Original Equipment Manufacture) designs, today every major catalog has at least one new twin shock frame available in a number of configurations.

Most of these frames will accept any Big Twin engine and many will take either a four or five speed transmission. Like the modern soft-tail frames, most manufacturers of twin-shock frames offer a wide-tire kit to accommodate the popular fat tire look.

HOW TO CHOOSE THE RIGHT ONE

As stated earlier, when it comes to building a bike from scratch the frame choice is one of the two most important decisions you will make. The frame decision will affect and be affected by your choice of an engine and your feelings on style and the way you will use the bike.

First you need to decide where you want the shocks, or if there should be any shocks at all. Once you've decided on the basic frame type, then you need to find the individual frame that's right for your project.

These fat-bob style tanks are stretched with the Nempco's stretching kits. Nempco

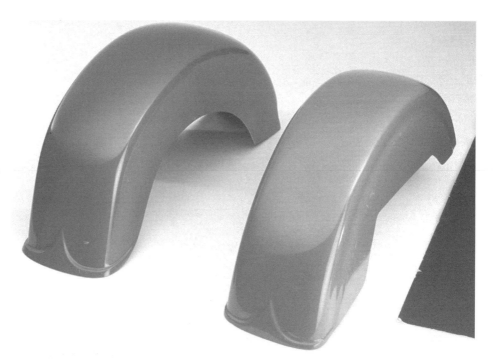

These composite fenders are among the new designs and materials currently being brought to the market. Drag Specialties.

This partially completed Mid-USA project is based on one of their new hard-tail frames. Mid-USA

This hard-tail frame is set up for a solid-mount Big Twin motor and fat-bob style tanks.

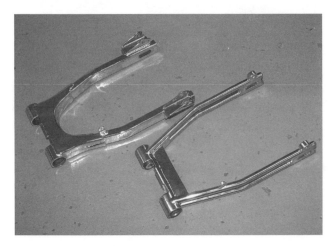

These are two of the many extra-wide swingarms currently being used on twin-shock frames - a twin-rail design from Tripoli and a modified FXR swingarm.

Because there are so many new frames on the market you've got more to chose from. Again, the frame you decide to take home from the shop or order through the catalog will affect and be affected by your other choices. I've tried to list the major criteria you might use to help narrow the field and find the right frame. You will also find examples of how the choice of one component will dictate the use of another and another.

In the soft-tail side of the market, the frames break down into OEM (original equipment manufacturer) and non-OEM configurations. The OEM designs closely mimic factory designs, and use factory dimensions and mounting points for tanks and sheet metal. Many of these frames even go so far as to include the webbing under the top tube so the terminal blocks on the factory wiring harness will snap into place.

The OEM style frame is nearly always the less-expensive option. Not only are these frames less expensive to buy, they are generally less expensive to equip as well. The frame will accept stock hardware and sheet metal, which tends to be the least expensive. What might be called custom frames with additional stretch require that you use a stretched tank(s) as well. Provisions for extra wide rear tires mean you must also use a matching extra wide fender.

Remember that some of the non-OEM frames are fairly "raw" and have no webbing to plug the wiring harness into and no mounting bosses for the Fat Bob tanks. This translates into more work and/or money.

On the twin-shock side of the market there are a few that mimic OEM frames, but most fall into a category that might be called, "generic twin-shock." Rather than use a duplicate of the factory frame most manufacturers on this side of the market build their own variation on the twin-shock theme. Among the more popular are the new Pro Street frames from Kenny Boyce and the always popular offerings from Arlen Ness. Yes, a true OEM-style frame would probably be cheaper, but very few builders seem to choose that route.

In picking a frame of this style you need to find a design that fits your goals for the bike. From short and stubby to long and sleek, there are plenty of these frames out there to chose from. If you can't find an example that fits your sense of style then you just aren't looking hard enough.

If what you want is a very compact strictly-business type of bike then buy a frame that's advertised as being "only 3/4 of an inch longer than an XL 883." If something long and sleek is more your style order one of Arlen's frames with five inches of stretch and a fork angle of 35 degrees.

FAT IS WHERE IT'S AT

The fat-tire look is very much in vogue among the custom bike set. Before assuming you need this new look consider all the information. Yes, many modern frames come with extra-wide swingarms and other provisions so builders can run a 170 or 180 series rear tire and retain the belt drive. But as Rob Carlson notes in his interview in Chapter One, the wide tire option usually adds to the cost of the project, both directly and indirectly.

Running a big tire in a V-Twin frame is not as easy as it sounds and often requires more than just a wide swingarm. The swingarm provides room for the tire, but there remains the larger problem of the tire running into the belt.

To provide room between the belt and tire, some frame manufacturers keep the rear wheel pulley lined up with the transmission pulley and move the wheel to the right slightly.

Two factory wide-glide triple trees, one of which has been "trimmed" to work on a frame designed for a narrow-glide fork.

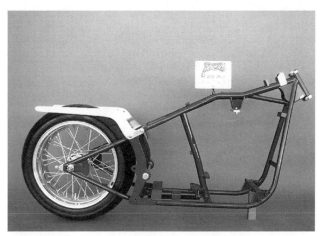

This Wide Drive soft-tail style chassis from Atlas bolts the engine solid to the frame and is designed to accept a wide rear tire and belt drive. Atlas

The top tube of this Kenny Boyce frame shows the three electrical plugs of the Softail harness, the self-cancelling module and the mount for the rubber-mount fat-bob tanks.

This mock-up in Donnie Smith's shop shows a Kenny Boyce framed bike being assembled and fabricated. Note the hand -formed seat pad which will then be upholstered.

The close-up shows the engine and transmission in a typical soft-tail style frame before the inner and outer primary are bolted on.

This leaves the front and rear wheels offset slightly from one another. This doesn't seem to cause any handling problems as long as the wheel offset is small, (like a quarter inch) though the degree to which it affects the handling depends on who you talk to. This type of offset does affect procedures used for checking alignment of the wheels.

The other basic option is to leave the rear wheel lined up with the front wheel and move the wheel pulley to the left. Now you have to move the transmission pulley over to the left to line up with the wheel pulley. Moving the transmission pulley to the left means moving the transmission, or the engine and transmission, to the left as well. Most frames move the engine and transmission to the left a relatively small amount so the impact on the bike's balance is minimal. Other frames however, are said to move the engine and transmission so far to the left that there is a noticeable affect on the balance.

No matter which frame you chose, ask the manufacturer or dealer for a recommendation for the wheel and spacers they use to get everything lined up correctly. It might save plenty of otherwise tedious work getting the driveline lined up correctly.

The best way to get that

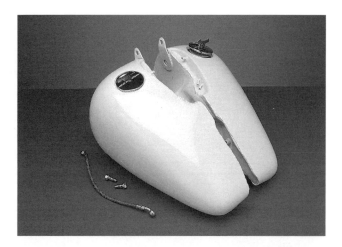

Fat-bob style tanks come in 3-1/2 and 5 gallon (and some 6 gallon) models. These 5 gallon rubber-mount tanks will give your ride a much fatter look than the smaller variety. Custom Chrome.

Nearly all scratch-built bikes are based on Big Twin engines - this soft-tail Sportster chassis from Atlas, however, is designed to accept all late-model Sportster engine and transmission units. Atlas

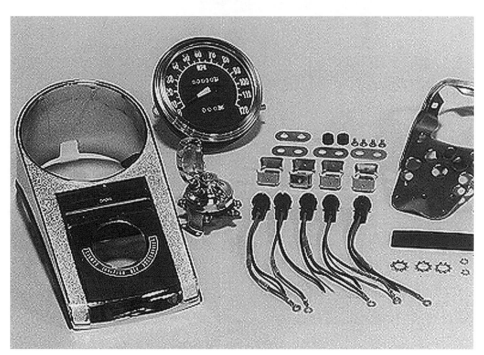

Buying parts in kits save time chasing around town in search of a missing bolt or bracket. For example, you can buy a complete kit for the dash with the base, speedo and cover. Mid-USA

31

These solid-mount fat-boy style tanks are available in 3-1/2 and 5 gallon models. Drag Specialties

big fat meat in the bike and get everything to line up depends on who you talk to. There seems to be a lot of "grey" material here in the sense that absolutes are hard to find. In your struggle to find the right fat-frame ask plenty of questions before you buy into the Pro Street look.

HOW TO DECIDE

No matter which style of frame you want there are plenty to choose from and new offerings nearly every week. Do not assume that all frames are of equal quality. If you hang around the shops that have been building bikes for a long time you will hear plenty of horror stories. Motor mounts that weren't true or didn't line up with the transmission mount or fork necks that were so crooked they put the front wheel an inch off to one side. Most of the frames out there *are* good, but you don't want to bring home one of the few exceptions. It's up to you to find a few that fit your budget and style, whether that's a twin-shock design or a fat-bob style. Once you have it narrowed down to a few possibilities, do a bit more homework and research to determine which of those are the very best. Remember, this is the foundation for the project, the bricks and concrete everything else is built on.

Among the new offerings from Arlen Ness is this long stretched aluminum gas tank. Arlen Ness Inc.

POWDER COATING

A good bike should be built to ride, not sit in splendor in the garage. The goal then is to build something that looks great and will continue to look great even as the miles pile up on the odometer. We all want a beautiful paint job and we hate rock chips. While a few chips might give your bike the "ridden" look, after a certain point you end up with the ridden-to-death look instead. The way out of this dilemma is through the use of good materials - paints that look good yet have the durability to laugh in the face of a gravel road.

It might sound impossible, but such a finish does exist. Powder coating is the answer to many a biker's prayers. How tough is a powder coated paint job? Durable enough that you can take a hammer and beat

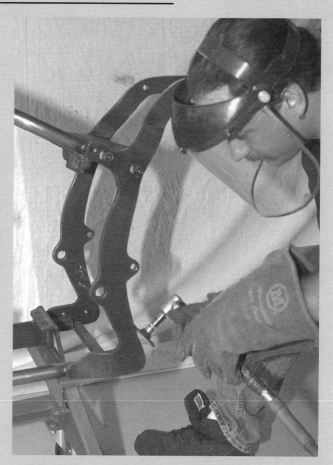

Before powder coating this frame, or any kind of painting, it's a good idea to clean up as many of the rough edges as possible. Be careful, however, not to get too energetic grinding on the welds that hold the frame together.

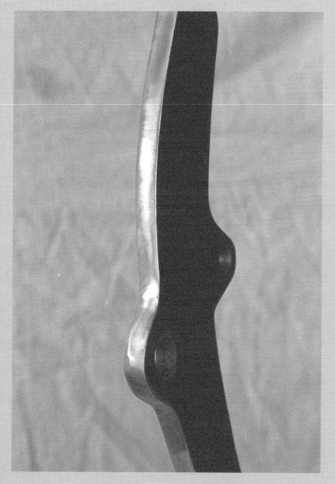

These large plates on the soft-tail style frame are often a little rough around the edges. After working them over with the small grinder the edges look much more finished.

the hell out of a powder coated panel (a display panel!). The panel will dent long before the paint chips off.

Though you can powder coat most metals, this relatively new process has caught on as the hot ticket for painting frames and other chassis components. In order to get a bettor idea of what's really involved in powder coating, I followed along as a new frame from M-C Specialties received the powder coating process at Best Coat in Blaine, Minnesota. Dick White, operator and part-owner of Best Coat, started the day by explaining the basic ground rules for powder coating.

Like nearly any painting operation the most important part of the job is the preparation. This means a good shop must first remove all the old paint or rust before they can start on the actual coating.

Here's the frame from Chapter 8. The first step is a dip in the cleansing tank, then the actual powder coating starts. Note the plugs in the top and bottom of the neck.

Areas that are to remain bare metal, like the engine and transmission mounting pads - are masked off with special tape so no powder will adhere to the metal.

"We recommend that all parts be blasted using glass bead or fine sand media," explained Dick. "The surface should be smooth, like the finish that plastic blasting leaves. Some shops use other, more aggressive, media that leaves the surface too rough. If the surface is too rough the finish coat will be rough too, because powder coating will not cover any imperfections. A typical powder coat is only one and a half to two mils thick (one mil equals .001 inch)."

Nearly any metal part can be powder coated though the durability makes powder coating very popular for engine components and chassis parts. But before taking your heads or barrels down to the powder coating shop there are a few things to consider. "Keep in mind," explains Dick, "that the parts you bring in will be baked in an oven. The heat is hard on seals or non metallic parts, they all have to come out. And any oil in the pores of the metal will turn liquid and run, which may ruin the job."

The other common problem Dick sees occurs with rusty parts. "Even after you've eliminated the rust by whatever means you still have the rust pits to deal with. For filling rust pits you need to use an all-metal type of filler, something like Aluma-lead or All-metal. Proper use of this type filler will smooth out the rough surfaces allowing the powder coating to give you an equally smooth finish.

Powder coating doesn't stick well to chrome, the surface is so smooth the powder has nothing to adhere to. Dick likes to see people take the parts to a chrome shop

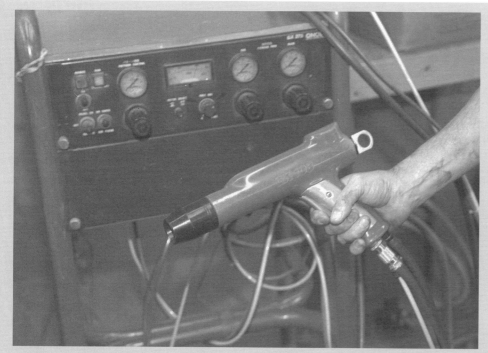

the gun during the application process causes the powder to attach itself to the frame. As Dick explains it, "The paint powder starts out in the hopper where air pressure moves it through the lines to the gun. The paint gun itself creates an electrostatic field so the powder particles pick up a high negative charge. Since the frame has a positive charge relative to the powder, the difference in potential between the frame and the powder causes the powder to attach itself to the frame's metal surface.

Applying the powder

Looking more like a timing light than a spray gun, the "spray" gun is connected to the electrical panel which controls the magnetic field and the voltage.

and have the chrome stripped off, or at least have the parts blasted so the surface has a little texture.

NOW, THE MOTORCYCLE FRAME

Following the short introductory lesson in powder coating Dick gets down to business with the new frame. The first step is a short dip of only a few minutes in the cleaning tank which contains approximately three percent phosphoric acid. This cleans off the surface oils and leaves a thin coating of iron phosphate, improving the adhesion of the powder coating.

After rinsing off the frame Dick puts it in the oven to bake for five minutes. This step dries the frame quickly and prevents any flash rusting. Before starting on the actual coating Dick plugs all the threaded holes and the neck so the threads aren't gummed up with the paint and so the fork bearing cups will fit correctly. He carefully masks off the motor mount areas using high temperature tape. That way there will be a good metal-to-metal connection between the engine and the frame, necessary for a good electrical connection and to ensure that the motor mounting bolts won't loosen later when the coating between the engine and frame eventually wears through from the constant vibration.

The powder Dick uses for our frame is a dry polyester powder. An electrostatic charge created by

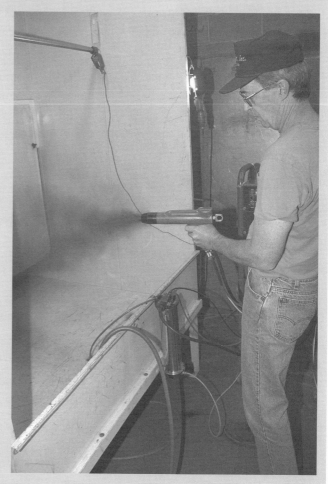

The spray gun puts out a soft mist of powder which is drawn into the "booth." Any powder that doesn't go on the object is collected at the back of the booth for disposal.

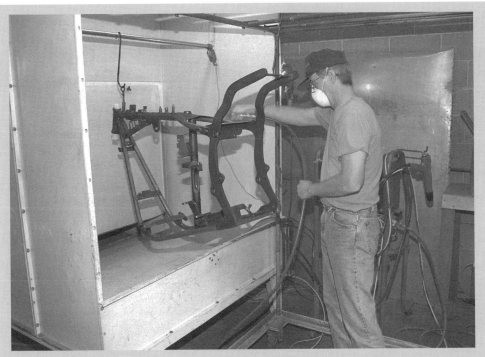

coat is much like a conventional spray paint operation, though the paint comes out of the gun in a soft cloud instead of a mist and drifts up and onto the frame in an eerie kind of slow motion. Because of the electrostatic attraction between the powder and the frame the cloud of pulverized paint surrounds the frame and actually wraps around the back side of the tubing. Any powder that doesn't stick to the frame is drawn into the booth and ends up in the dust trap at the back of the booth. Disposal of the dust is not a problem as it contains only non-toxic ingredients.

Though the electrostatic

Even though the powder is drawn to the object, it takes a good operator to make sure the material gets into all the little nooks and crannies of a frame.

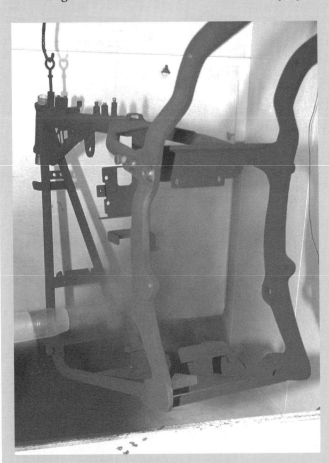

Here you can actually see the very fine powder as it drifts onto the frame. After the frame is completely coated it spends time in a large oven which bakes on the finish.

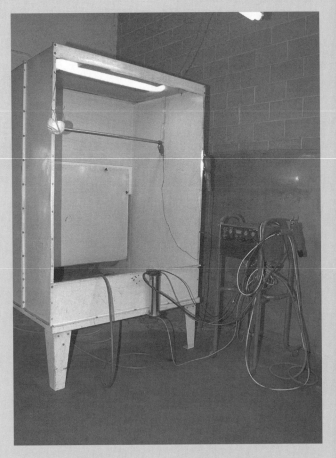

Small objects are suspended in the booth itself, while larger objects like our frame are mounted at the edge.

charge is what draws the powder to the frame, it's the bake cycle in the large oven that causes the powder to actually bond with the metal. The frame stays in the over for 35 minutes at 380 degrees. Dick explains that there are tests to ensure that the powder is fully cured and bonded to the metal. But in cases like our frame, where he does a number of similar jobs every week, no such test is necessary.

After 35 minutes in the oven the frame is allowed to cool and is then ready to assemble. The finish is very black and very glossy. The combination of super durable materials baked and bonded to the bare metal means this finish is extremely rock and bruise resistant.

If you want more than just a black frame, Dick (and most good powder coating operations) can provide metallics, textures and multiple coats including clearcoats and candy finishes. In cases where you want the sheet metal color to match the powder color Dick recommends that you have the parts powder coated first and then match the color of the powder coat with the liquid paint - as that is much easier than the reverse. As with any good quality powder coating operation Dick spends time with his customers to help them select the best color combinations and special effects from the many options available.

So if you're looking for an extremely durable finish for that new frame and swingarm consider powder coating. It's both colorful and durable.

After the powder coating Mike at M-C goes over all the threaded holes with a tap set. In addition to cleaning out any paint, he also repairs any holes that were damaged in shipping or mis-tapped at the factory.

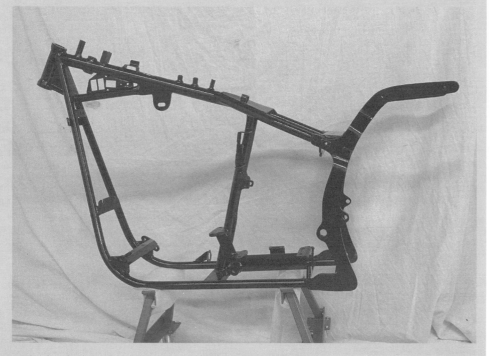

The finished product, very black, shiny and durable. Powder coating can also be clear coated for a deeper shine.

Chapter Three

Chassis Components

Find the right Fork, Shocks, Wheels, Tires and Brakes

So you've got the frame sitting on your work bench or hoist, and a pile of boxes from S&S, Harley-Davidson, Arlen Ness, and Custom Chrome in the corner. It's time now to buy and install the front fork and the rear suspension. Thus we have more questions: Like, what's a wide-glide or a narrow glide, how high off the ground should the frame be, and how does that translate into the length of the rear shocks.

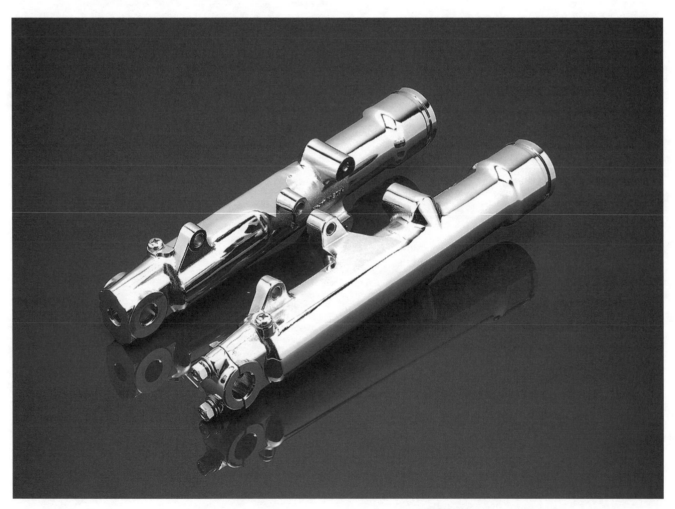

Designed for 41mm fork tubes, these lower legs feature mounting points for dual calipers, and are already pol-ished and chrome plated. Custom Chrome

START AT THE FRONT

Your choice of a fork assembly is dictated party by aesthetics and popular convention. Most soft-tail style bikes run a wide-glide fork while most (though not all) twin-shock bikes run narrow-glide forks.

If those choices are just too pedestrian, then there are more exotic upside-down forks from White Bros. and light-weight Ceriani forks available from Storz. For the purpose of this book the discussion will be limited to the fork offerings commonly found on late model Harley-Davidson motorcycles.

As long as you're building a new bike it only makes sense to buy a new fork. There are no "rebuilt" forks available, and there's no point in buying a used fork for a new bike. Besides, the lower triple tree has a number stamped in it that matches the bike it was originally shipped with so it could be a problem in the future.

Ordering the right fork tubes, legs and triple trees can be kind of confusing. And the more you look the worse it seems to become. There is rather a vast array of forks that have been used at one time or another by the factory. But let's limit the discussion to late model offerings, in which case the number of possible units is more reasonable.

In current use there are

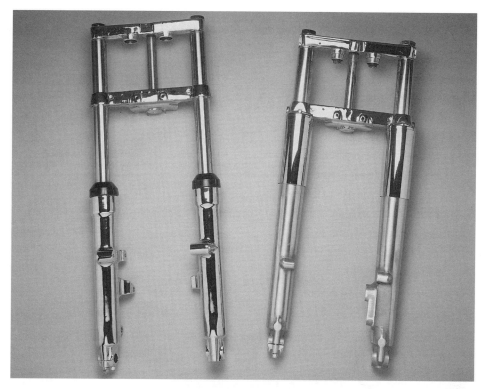

Many of the aftermarket fork assemblies are available with chrome plated lower legs, like the dual disc FLT on the left. Also shown is an earlier, single-disc FL assembly.

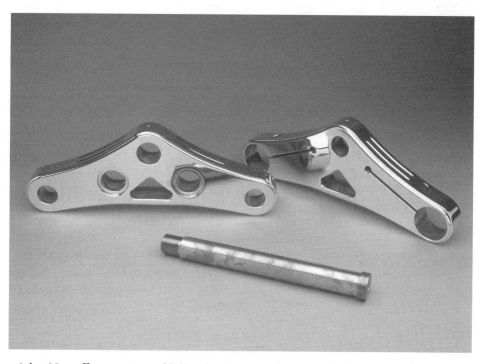

Arlen Ness offers a variety of billet aluminum triple trees including these wide glide models. Arlen Ness Inc.

39

two fork-tube diameters, 39mm and 41mm. The 39 mm, or narrow-glide, is used on Sportsters and some Dyna models. This fork assembly comes in three lengths with provisions for single or dual disc brakes.

The 41mm forks come in three basic versions, FLT, Softail Custom and Heritage (also Fat Boy). The FLT (or Dresser) tubes are the shortest, with Heritage coming next in length and Softail Custom being the longest of all. Of course

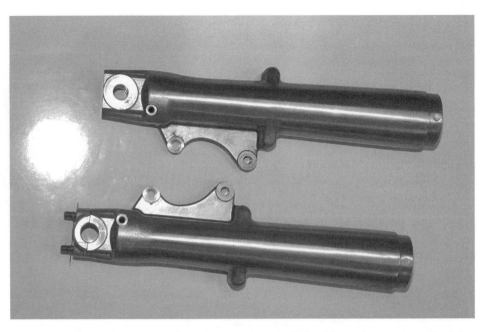

The easiest way to install dual front discs on a wide-glide front end is to be sure the lower legs you buy both have mounting points for the calipers - but not all factory front ends came with dual discs so you have to buy the right style.

This close up of the bike seen in Chapter 9 shows the trimmed lower triple tree (and the fork stop). Also note the serial numbers (or VIN) on the neck area. These numbers must remain readable after painting and possible molding of the frame.

longer and (sometimes) shorter tubes are available in most styles from the various aftermarket companies. Or you can call Forking by Frank for a custom tube of any length.

If you want dual discs on a 41mm fork, you either have to run FL style lower fork legs with factory attaching points for the calipers or use aftermarket calipers with their own mounting system.

WHICH ONE IS RIGHT FOR YOU?

The neck and fork stem bearings are the same on all late model Big Twin bikes, so in theory any triple tree should work on any frame - but of course it's not that simple.

Most FXR-style frames are set up to run 39mm narrow-glide forks. When you try to put a set of factory wide-glide triple trees on one of these frames part of the lower triple tree contacts the down-tubes just below the neck. The way out of this dilemma is found by trimming away material (the lock tab and surrounding metal) from the stock wide-glide triple tree so it can be substituted for the narrow-glide triple tree. There is no similar problem when bolting a narrow-glide onto a frame that normally runs a wide-glide fork assembly.

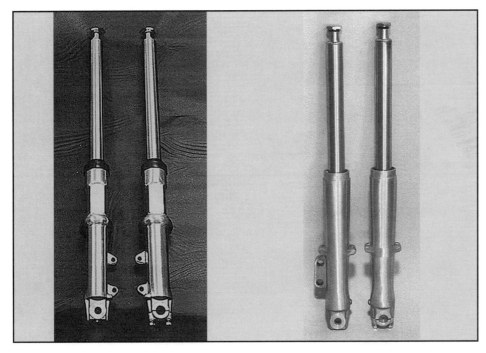

and what are your choices for triple trees. You also need to know where the fork stop is. Is it a tab on the lower front part of the neck, and is it meant to work with the tabs built into some factory lower trees? There is no point in reinventing the wheel. Use parts that are designed to work together.

HOW LONG IS TOO LONG?

How long the fork tubes need to be will be affected by a number of

Among the wide variety of forks available for your new ride are these wide-glide assemblies - both the FXWG style and single-disc FL style. Mid-USA

If you like the looks of the 39mm fork legs but want a wide-glide front end, you can combine the two with aftermarket triple trees like those from Arlen Ness. These billet trees allow you to run 39mm fork legs in a wide-glide configuration

Once you've decided whether to run a wide-glide or narrow-glide you still need to decide how long the tubes should be and, in some cases, which style of tube best fits your situation.

All the components that make up the front end of the bike must be designed (or modified) to work with all the other parts. A wide-glide fork will require the proper wheel hub, or at least the right spacers. You need to know which style of fork stop the frame manufacturer designed into the frame and whether or not that stop will work with the triple trees you plan to use. The factory wide-glide trees, for example, have the stops built into the lower triple trees.

Confusing? Yes, but all of this can be unraveled if you will first spend some time reading any material that came with your frame. The next stop in the information highway is the frame manufacturer or the shop where you bought the frame. Ask what they recommend for a fork assembly

Note the molded frame and springer fork.

41

factors: the ride height, the fork design, the rake and the wheels you have chosen. There is no simple slide-rule or computer program for determining the right fork length. And setting up a frame on your hoist at ride height is harder than it might sound.

The place to start is again with the frame manufacturer and the shop that sold you the frame. If you plan to run a standard fork then someone should be able to tell you what length

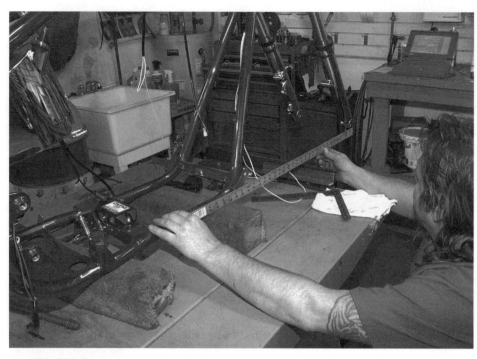

Richard from Minneapolis Custom Cycle uses a yard stick to determine the relationship between the fork length and ride height.

In addition to factory front ends, a variety of more expensive fork assemblies are available like this upside-down Ceriani front end on Steve Laugtug's bike.

tube they typically run and where that puts the bike in terms of ride height.

RIDE HEIGHT

At Minneapolis Custom Cycle, they like to have nearly seven inches of clearance between the bottom of the frame tubes and the ground. As Richard Rohda, mechanic at the shop explains, "We like to run enough ground clearance that you can run the bike into a curve and not worry about dragging parts."

Of course most factory Softails don't have that much clearance - and riders are lowering those bikes still further. The low-and-slow crowd often get by with as little as four inches of clearance between the frame and terra firma. It's another of those decisions affected by the way you intend to ride the bike. Don't slam it to the ground if you intend to chase Ninja-bikes down canyon roads.

When it comes to setting up the bike initially it's a good idea to follow the advice of the frame manufacturer or shop where you bought the bike. Let them suggest a fork assembly and tube length, probably something that's easy to get and doesn't require cutting or ordering tubes in an unusual length. Avoid the temptation to "slam" this new

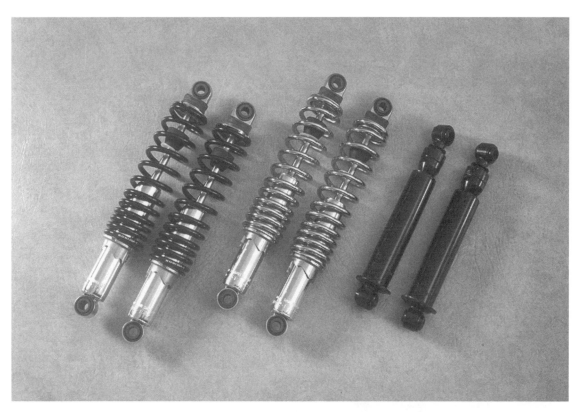

Shock absorbers and springs for twin-shock bikes come in every style, length and price range imaginable. Figure out the length first, then how much spring you need and finally what price range works.

One way to lower your soft-tail frame is to install these shorter rear shocks from Progressive Suspension. Drag Specialties

ride. After all you can probably lower it later more easily than you can raise it if you built it too low.

ANATOMY OF A SHOCK ABSORBER

Yes, it might look like a simple tube filled with oil - but in reality a modern shock absorber is a very complex piece of equipment.

Looking at the shape of a shock absorber it's easy to imagine the piston attached to the pushrod moving through a cylinder filled

Some shocks require that you use a flanged washer as shown, be sure the flange is on the outside and not the inside of the shock.

with oil.

Most shocks have a pair of valves located on the piston head. As the piston moves into the cylinder on compression a valve is unseated to open an orifice or series of orifices and the oil passes through those little openings. When the shock goes into rebound that first valve is closed and a different valve opens to allow the piston to move through the cylinder in the opposite direction with the oil passing through a different set of openings.

Premium shocks allow the user to adjust the damping with some kind of external screw or knob

Premium shocks allow the user to adjust the damping (in compression only, or in both compression and rebound) with some kind of external screw or knob - effectively changing the sizes of the holes that the fluid passes through.

The viscosity of the oil and the size of the

No longer in production, this style of 41mm wide-glide front end is still available in the aftermarket.

It's helps to get the bike close to the actual ride height during the mock-up stage so you can accurately judge the way all the parts "fit" the bike and each other.

rapidly it cavitates and soon there are air bubbles mixed with the oil. This aerated oil and air mixture isn't really oil at all. In this condition the shock is said to have "faded" and contributes almost nothing to the control of the suspension.

Most of the problems encountered by a shock working overtime are overcome by the features found on most premium shock absorber designs. First, everything is a little larger

holes that the oil passes through are the major factors affecting the stiffness of a particular shock absorber. By using different orifices for compression and rebound a manufacturer is able to provide one level of stiffness on compression and another on rebound. Some shock absorbers are valved closer to fifty-fifty (the same on compression and rebound).

In this condition the shock is said to have "faded" and contributes almost nothing to the control of the suspension.

Most original equipment shock absorbers work just fine until you ride down a washboard gravel road at high speed. Soon the shock absorber pistons are moving through the fluid so fast and changing direction so often that a great deal of heat is created. The heat tends to change the viscosity of the oil, causing it to become thinner and reducing the effective stiffness of the shocks. Worse, as the piston changes direction

On a twin-shock frame the length of the rear shock determines the height. At Minneapolis Custom Cycle they use a 12 or 13 inch shock because the don't want them too low.

Similar to a wheel design seen earlier in the book, this is a good example of the infinite number of possibilities available to billet wheel designers. Arlen Ness Inc.

and built to withstand additional loads. To better handle the heat the amount of oil may be increased. For better cooling the body of the shock can be made of aluminum to take advantage of aluminum's ability to quickly dissipate heat to the surrounding air. To reduce the tendency toward cavitation and the aeration of the oil a pressure chamber is built into the shock filled with nitrogen gas. By pressurizing the oil the tendency toward aeration is reduced. Much the way pressurizing an automotive cooling system raises the boiling point of the antifreeze.

Shocks on the rear of twin-shock style bikes come wrapped in a spring, while soft-tail style suspension puts the spring and shock in one sealed housing. Springs are rated in pounds per inch, or how far the spring will compress under a given load. Placement of the shock pivots affects the leverage with which the shock/spring unit holds up the bike, so the right spring for one frame and swingarm combination isn't necessarily the right one for a different combination.

WHICH ONE

On a twin-shock bike the length of the shock can be used to raise or lower the bike at the rear. Before buying rear shocks for this style of bike you need to know the length, eye to eye, and the spring rate.

Remember that the spring rate you need is affected by your weight and

These are just two of the designs available from Sturgis Wheel Company. Both are cast from 356 aluminum before being finished on a CNC mill. Mid-USA

whether or not you intend to ride double. When you ask for a recommendation for shock length get one for the recommended spring rate as well.

Now you need to plug the length and spring rate into a coil-over shock that has the quality, looks and price that makes it the right shock for you.

For a soft-tail style frame there are a number of shocks available, some of which allow the owner to adjust the ride height. Or you can order premium gas-charged shocks for your soft-tail chassis and install one of the popular lowering kits from White Bros. or one of the other aftermarket companies. There is even an adjustable torsion bar suspension kit available that is said to provide a better overall ride with less bottoming over bumps.

This Panhead chopper with springer fork and 21 inch wheel is an obvious example of the need to match the fork and wheel to the style of the bike.

WHEELS

The most common wheel sizes used on V-Twin powered motorcycles are 21, 19 and 16 for the front, and 16 for the rear. With the phenomenal growth in the custom wheel market the "standard" diameters have grown to include 18 and 17 for the rear. In particular, while stock late model bikes commonly run a 130/90x16 inch rear tire, the current trend is to larger rubber for the "fat and fast" look. Many riders are replacing the 130 series rear tires with 140 and larger tires. The really fat sizes like 170, 180 and even 200 are available in 17 and 18 inch diameters.

How fat that rear rubber should be is another decision that must be made early in the planning stage. Running anything wider than 140 requires off-set kits and/or frames designed to accommodate the big tires. If fat is where it's at, buy your

Just a few of the forged aluminum designs available in all the popular sizes, polished or in chrome plate. Custom Chrome.

With this Power House frame you can have a soft-tail style frame with a fat rear tire and belt drive. Mid-USA

frame and swingarm accordingly (see Chapter Two for more on wide tire options).

Consider that to run a tire even one size larger than stock in an OEM style frame often requires that the tire be moved to the right by machining away part of the caliper mount so there's room between the tire and the belt. In effect this leaves the rear tire offset slightly as compared to the front. Whether or not this is a serious problem depends on who you talk to, but it's one more thing to think about as you plan the new motorcycle. The other basic option in this regard is to trade in the belt for a chain which leaves more room for the wider rear tire.

Don't forget that the stock and OEM style fenders are designed for OEM sized tires. Even one size bigger might well rub on the inside of the fender, a situation that should be avoided at all costs.

Front tires tend to be one of three sizes: 16, 19 or 21. Dressers and "fat" bikes look good with the 16 inch tires while almost everything else seems to work best with the 19 inch tire and wheel combination. 21 inch tires look good on springers and in certain other situations, though some experienced riders say that a bike handles better with a 19 than with a 21 inch front tire (one more thing to argue about at the saloon).

Shown is a FXR transmission which will have the rear mount shaved on the left side (with the tool in the lower portion of the photo). The spacer is used on the right side of the mount to make up for the lost material.

In the end the bike's style will dictate the size of the tire. But choosing the wheels and tires is another example of decisions that must be made in concert with all the other choices. A wide-glide fork will require the correct wheel hub. A 21 inch wheel in place of a 19 will affect the ride height, which in turn affects your fork choice.

When you buy the wheels be sure to tell the dealer or counter person as much as you can about the bike. If it's a narrow glide fork with dual disc and you want to run a 90/90x19, tell them exactly that.

BRAKES

When it comes to building a new bike we all want the machine to run fast. We should likewise take the time to make sure it stops just as fast.

There is rather a bewildering bunch of brake calipers and master cylinders on the market these days. Rather than list each caliper, I've chosen to offer the following guidelines and tips on brake systems in general and choosing the right overall system in particular.

Brakes are essentially heat machines - converting the moving or kinetic energy of your motorcycle to heat. When planning how much brakes to buy it might be instructive to remember that when you double the speed of a vehicle you create four times the kinetic energy. When buying brakes for a

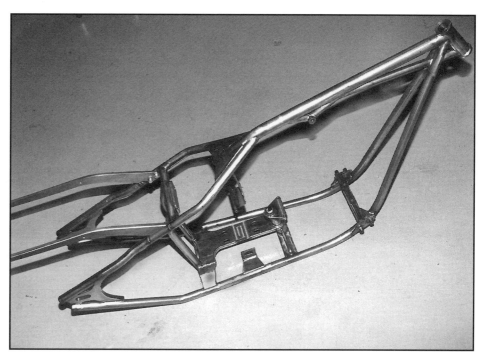

This hardtail frame is a new offering from Chrome Specialties. Designed by Donnie Smith, the frame will accept a 200 series rear tire and is available with five inches of stretch.

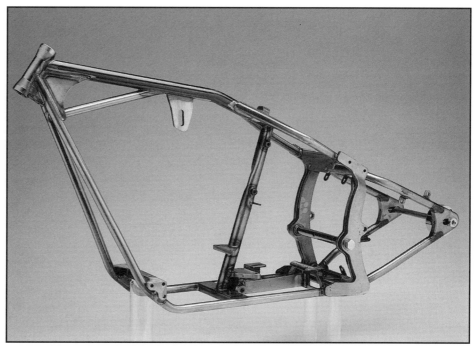

This "longneck" frame from Santee features 3 inches of stretch in the top tube, not the lower downtubes. Comes with a wide swingarm to accept a 180 rear tire with belt drive. Can be ordered with or without mounts for flatside tanks. CCI

49

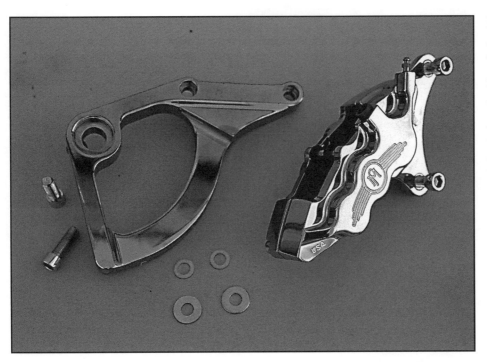

The brake caliper is one of the new six-piston designs from Performance Machine, while the rear caliper bracket is a fabricated piece from McAllister Motorcycles.

high performance motorcycle more is usually better. This means more rotor surface area, more pistons per caliper (usually with larger pads as well) and in some cases, more calipers. The down-side to the more-brakes-are-better theory is the expense, complexity and additional unsprung weight.

Because the front wheel has something like seventy percent (or more) of the stopping power, spend the bulk of your brake budget on the front wheel. In terms of increasing the stopping power of a motorcycle, the simplest and most effective improvement is the addition of another caliper and rotor to a single-disc front end. This decision should be made during the planning stages so you get the right fork legs, calipers and brackets.

As an engineer from Performance Machine told me years ago, you need to consider what the bike will be used for and then chose the brake system accordingly. Canyon racers will need different brakes than boulevard cruisers. The addition of four-piston calipers gives an improvement of 35 percent over the braking performance of factory calipers. The four piston caliper uses a bigger brake pad and two pistons per pad to evenly push the pad against the spinning rotor. By switching to larger diameter rotors the performance is further improved - the larger rotors provide more braking sur-

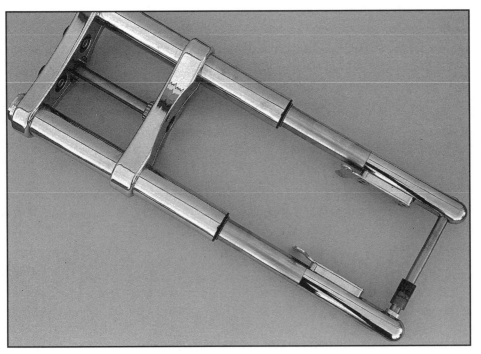

Inverted forks offer several design advantages, including reduced flex and unsprung weight. This example is from Spyke and features provision for one or two calipers, and an easy ride height adjustment.

face as well as more leverage for the caliper.

Most rotors are stainless steel, polished stainless rotors are available for those who need all the extra glitter. Experienced builders warn of having the rotors chrome plated. It may look great but the chrome surface is so smooth that the brake pads can't grab hold of it and stopping power suffers in the extreme.

Brake pads too come in a variety of materials and styles. Use the wrong pad material on an iron rotor and the pad will cut into the rotor. So ask the shop where you buy your parts to ensure a good match between the pads and rotors.

While you're asking questions and feeling humble ask which master cylinder you need to use with the new calipers. If the hydraulic ratios aren't correctly matched between the master cylinder and calipers you could end up with high effort brakes, or a master cylinder with too small a piston that doesn't displace enough fluid to fully apply the brakes. Two sizes of front master cylinder piston are commonly available: 5/8 and 3/4 inch diameter, with 3/4 being the preferred size for dual disc applications. Again, check with the salesperson to be sure you match the caliper(s) to the master cylinder.

Braided brake lines are

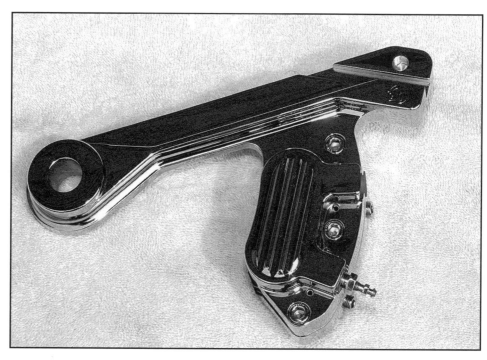

GMA has a number of new designs on the market, including this four-piston rear caliper that comes with integral bracket and a chrome plated finish.

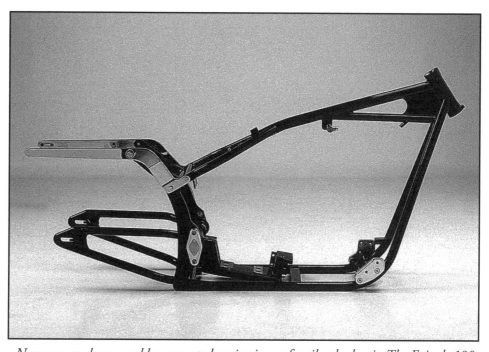

Now you can have a rubber mounted engine in a soft-tail style chassis. The Episode 180 from Daytec/Arlen Ness combines soft-tail suspension and styling with a rubber-mounted engine and transmission. Available in 2 and 5 inches of stretch with a 34 degree rake. Arlen Ness

Don't neglect the outside of your engine when designing the bike. Complete chrome plated billet cover sets are available for both Evo and Twin-cam engines. Arlen Ness

often used to plumb the new brake system. They have the advantage of not expanding under pressure the way rubber hoses do. The braided lines have a very nice, business-like look to them that often complements a custom motorcycle. Perhaps the major advantage of braided lines is the fact that most shops can make them up from scratch in nearly any length with any combination of fittings. The downside to all this improved performance is the tendency of braided lines to act like a saw on that fresh paint job, so be sure to clamp the lines securely or contain them in shrink wrap the way Kokesh did with the bike they built (see Chapter Seven).

When you install the calipers use the correct mounting brackets and bolts, because the full force of a panic stop is transmitted from the caliper to the chassis through the caliper mounting bracket and bolts. Also be sure the caliper is centered over the rotor (this is not a concern with factory, one-piston calipers). Many caliper kits come with spacers that can be used between the caliper and the mounting bracket to locate the caliper.

Once you have all the new brake components hung on that great looking bike of yours the only thing left is to fill it with brake fluid and bleed the system.

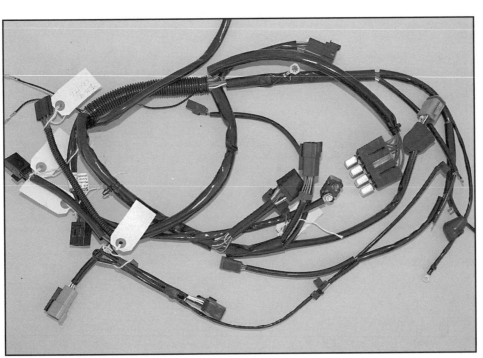

The water-proof harness shown here is used on many '95 and later H-D products. Note the nice connectors and the way the 4 circuit breakers are grouped together. Your choice of a harness will affect your choice of other components like the base for the dash.

Fahrenheit, dry), no tendency to absorb water and no reaction when spilled on a painted surface. It costs more and is reputed to be slightly compressible, though no one seems to notice any difference in "feel" after switching to silicone fluid. The higher cost seems a small price to pay for such a much better product. No matter which fluid you decide to use, stick with it and do not mix one brake fluid type with another.

This left side rear brake uses a large diameter rotor that bolts to the inside of the pulley, combined with a four-piston aluminum caliper and support bracket.

So you go to the local store only to find that there are at least three different types of brake fluid available for your new ride.

What we call brake fluid is simply a very specialized hydraulic fluid. One that operates in a very dirty environment and must withstand very high temperatures without boiling. When brake fluid boils the fluid becomes a gas (a compressible material). The rider senses this as a very soft or spongy feeling brake lever or pedal. Brake fluid must stay viscous at nearly any temperature and resist boiling up to 400 degrees Fahrenheit.

There are three grades of brake fluid commonly available, DOT 3, DOT 4 and DOT 5. DOT 3 and 4 are glycol-based fluids with dry boiling points of 401 and 446 degrees Fahrenheit respectively. Either fluid is suitable for use in disc brake systems. There are two basic problems with DOT 3 and DOT 4 brake fluids: They tend to absorb water from the environment (they are hydroscopic) and they attack most paints.

The answer to the problems inherent in DOT 3 and 4 brake fluids are overcome by DOT 5 brake fluid. DOT 5 fluid is silicone based, meaning a higher boiling point (500 degrees

TP Eng. offers a series of complete engines with either a 3-5/8 or 4 inch bore. Most of the components are manufactured in-house, including cases, cylinders, pistons and heads. These engines use CNC machined parts and counter-sunk bolt holes wherever possible.

Chapter Four

V-Twin and Transmission

Choose the right engine and drivetrain

If you cut to the quick, a motorcycle is really nothing more than a frame and engine, with a gas tank to feed the engine and a wheel at either end. The engine is not only the largest piece of machinery but the most expensive single item as well.

The range of possible V-Twin engines (and the options for each one of those engines) is large and growing larger by the day. On the modest end there's always the complete 80 or 88 cubic inch motor from Harley-Davidson. Or you can pull out the stops and buy 120 or more cubic inches with offerings from the aftermarket.

Currently, most aftermarket bikes are based on evo-

From Zipper's Performance comes their Big-Block series. All use a 3-13/16 inch bore combined with various stroker crankshafts to achieve displacements of 97, 102 and

105 cubic inches. These are complete engines, test run before delivery. The 102 dynos at over 120 pounds of torque and nearly 120 horsepower. Zipper's

Among the complete engines on the market is this assembly from Custom Chrome. These engines have been redesigned on sophisticated CAD equipment to incorporate the latest in engine technology and come in 88 and 100 cubic inches. CCI

style engines, though a few frames are starting to appear that will accept the new twin-cam (non B-style) engine. Donnie Smith is working on a rear engine mounting plate that would adapt a twin-cam into one of their CSI frames (as seen in Chapter 7). As Donnie explains, "the center-line distances are the same (engine to transmission) but you have to machine a little metal off the rear of the engine case to make it fit our frame."

If a twin-cam is what you've got to have for power, check around, the aftermarket is sure to provide a way to install the new factory motor in the old-style frames.

THE RIGHT ONE FOR YOU

This section is not intended as a complete buyer's guide, but rather as an overview of some of the offerings currently on the market and some tips as to how you might chose the right one. Picking the motor is the second most important decision you will make regarding the new bike, no one but you can do it. Take your time and do plenty or research before making a final decision. If you ask Tom Pirone from TP Engineering how to pick an engine, his answer is simple. "You have to ask yourself, how do I ride. Am I a drag racer or a highway rider?"

Included in the overall budget for the bike should be dollar figure for the engine. This figure, combined with the type of riding you intend to do and perhaps some good advice from a good shop or engine builder (not the advice that comes so freely at the local tavern), will lead you to the motor that's right for you.

In a general sense more money gets you more motor, but the relationships between horsepower (and torque) and the cost aren't strictly logical or linear. Assuming you're going to buy a new engine, the cheapest you can get a complete engine is currently somewhere between three and five thousand dollars. Your options at that entry level include complete crate motors from your local Harley-Davidson dealer, a dis-assembled engine from a manufacturer like S&S, an engine "kit" from one of the aftermarket suppliers or an engine assembled from a combination of aftermarket and factory parts. If you're willing to spend five or six thousand dollars, a much larger range of complete and nearly complete engines become available. Everything from one of the new complete engines from C.C.I. to a complete and assembled big-bore

Always an industry leader, S&S offers a full range of complete engines with the 4 inch bore. Possible displacements range up to 113 cubic inches (4-1/2 inch stroke). Engines can be purchased complete or as a kit to make painting and polishing easier. S&S

These four inch pistons from TP Engineering use a new webbing design to better support the skirt and help the pistons stand up to the added loads encountered with a 4 inch bore engine.

The aftermarket has been quick to offer high performance parts for the Twin-cam engine. These camshafts from Head Quarters use a .600 inch lift and 246 degree cam for the intake and .530 inch and 256 degree cam for the exhaust. Head Quarters

Stock Twin-cam heads are said to breathe poorly, a problem easily solved with the installation of these ported castings from Head Quarters. Heads come complete with a radius valve job, and new valves, guides, springs and seals. Head Quarters.

engine from S&S, TP Engineering, Zippers and a few more.

This whole business of choosing the right engine for your bike is filled with controversy and confusion. For first-time buyers it really helps to find a well respected shop and lean on them for some guidance.

POWER, POWER

If a mild 80 cubic inch cubic inch V-Twin just won't do it for your personal two-wheeled hot rod, then give serious thought to how much power you really want - and how much you're willing to spend to get that power. Remember too that there is no silver bullet. Good power comes through a combination of parts that achieve a certain mechanical harmony. A given camshaft, whether it's from Andrews or Screamin' Eagle, won't produce significant increases by itself.

The camshaft or carburetor you chose needs to be chosen in consideration with the other parts you intend to use. Most experienced engine builders can lay out various "stages" of engines that they have experience building. Each stage is based on a combination of parts that work together to provide a certain level of performance.

In searching for the right engine remember that you want more than just horsepower. You need torque too and you need to have both available in the RPM range where real people ride. An engine with 110 horses isn't much good on the street if all that power doesn't really come on until 6000 RPM. Big carburetors and drag pipes might provide good top-end power, but most of us need good low and mid-range power. Part of the beauty of the new big-block engines with 96, 100 or 107 cubic inches is the fact that that all those cubics create substantial amounts of torque and horsepower - all at real-world RPM levels.

Before putting down your hard-earned cash be sure to consider all your options. Remember, anything that seems too good to be true probably is, and a bike that doesn't run consistently isn't worth a damn no matter how fast it is.

A COMPUTERIZED CRYSTAL BALL

Until recently it was pretty tough to predict the exact outcome of a given combination of parts - unless the combination was one the engine builder had already used. And a package of parts that worked good in a 80 cubic inch engine with 10:1 compression might not work so well with an 89 cubic inch engine with 9:1 compression.

Wouldn't it be nice if you or I could start off with the basic engine we think we need and then experiment on paper with the different camshafts, carburetors and compression ratios. Instead of gambling that some new cam profile from Andrews of Sifton will work with the rest of the engine we could "dyno" the engine - with that new camshaft - on paper.

Well due to the wonders of technology anyone with a decent computer and the right software can do exactly that. Lee Wickstrom, engine builder for Kokesh Motorcycle Accessories and owner/builder of the world's quickest gasoline-powered Knucklehead, provided a demonstration of a software package from Walters Technology (available through Mid-USA). Lee has used this package to predict the outcome of various engines built both in the Kokesh shop and also at his home shop.

Complete kits are available to upgrade that stock Twin-cam. Shown is a complete kit with pistons of your choice, big bore cylinders and re-worked heads. Head Quarters

Designed by a pair of GM powertrain engineers, the Baker 6-speed transmission uses a .86 to 1 overdrive 6th, for a drop of 500 RPM at 80 MPH (a second overdrive ratio will soon be available). The transmission is manufactured in the US of A, including the full-width gears cut by Andrews.

```
FILE : COMB2
BORE DIA.        3.498            FLOW CORRECTION  13 CFM
STROKE LENGTH    4.250
ROD LENGTH       7.439            ROD/STROKE RATIO  1.75:1
NO. CYLINDERS    2
CUBIC INCH --------------- 81.69

COMBUSTION CHAMBER CC = 79.4  QUENCH CC =  0.0  TOTAL CC = 79.4
        COMPRESSION RATIO 9.4:1
                                        HEAD          PISTON VELOCITY
    *****CRANKSHAFT HORSEPOWER*****     C.F.M.    |***************|
   R.P.M.    H.P.   PER CYL. PER C.I. TORQUE REQ.@10  VE    MAX     AVG.
    3000    47.15    23.58    0.6     82.5    69.3   97%  3472.22  2125.00
    3500    59.58    29.79    0.7     89.4    80.3  106%  4050.92  2479.17
    4000    69.76    34.88    0.9     91.6    91.5  108%  4629.62  2833.33
    4500    81.35    40.68    1.0     94.9   102.9  112%  5208.32  3187.50
    5000    92.79    46.40    1.1     97.5   116.4  115%  5787.03  3541.67
    5500    99.78    49.89    1.2     95.3   128.5  113%  6365.73  3895.83
    6000   104.63    52.32    1.3     91.6   139.7  108%  6944.43  4250.00
    6500   104.09    52.05    1.3     84.1   153.0   99%  7523.13  4604.17
-----------------------------------------------------------------------------
           OPEN / CLOSE   DURATION   VALVE LIFT   LOBE CENTER  ROCKER RATIO
INTAKE     16.0 / 44.0     240.0    NET.326 .530    104.0       1.625:1
EXHAUST    44.0 / 16.0     240.0    NET.326 .530    104.0       1.625:1
                                     OVERLAP
           OVERLAP        [ PERCENTAGE ]        LOBE SEPARATION ANGLE
            32.0          [  5.0 % ]                   104.0
CAMSHAFT DESCRIPTION :
V THUNDER 3030 BY COMPETITION CAMS  STRONG MIDRANGE, GOOD ROLL ON IN HIGH GEAR.
CARB, PIPES AND HEADWORK.

PERCENTAGE OF CAMSHAFT OCCUPYING CYLINDER  113.0 PERCENT
110% TO 120%:MEDIUM PERCENTAGE.GOOD HIGH PERFORMANCE STREET, MID TO TOP END.

ESTIMATED STATIC COMPRESSION RANGE 151.2 PSI
145 TO 165 PSI:MODIFIED STREET MOTORS.DESIRABLE FOR H.P. STREET MOTORS.
-----------------------------------------------------------------------------

CYLINDER HEAD [CFM] FLOW CHART REQUIREMENTS TO OBTAIN ESTIMATED HORSEPOWER

     TOTAL         INT.        EXH.        INT.        EXH.
   VALVE LIFT    CFM @ 10    CFM @ 10    CFM @ 25    CFM @ 25
     .100          39.4        29.6        62.3        46.7
     .200          78.8        59.1       124.5        93.4
     .300         112.6        84.5       177.9       133.4
     .400         140.8       105.6       222.4       166.8
     .530         153.0       114.8       241.7       181.3

CARBURETOR FLOW REQUIREMENTS AT 10.0 INCH   149.1 C.F.M
```

Chart #2: This is one of the engine packages laid out by Lee Wickstrom, intended to illustrate the use of the Walters software as well as some logical engine choices that you might consider as you search for the right engine. This first package is what you might call a "strong-street 80." The 80 cubic inch engine uses a carburetor that will flow enough air (any good aftermarket carb would probably work here) coupled to factory heads that have been shaved .090 inches and given a good port job. The camshaft is a V Thunder 3030 from Competition Cams said to give "Strong midrange and good roll-on. The cam specifications are: 240 degrees of duration and .530 inches of lift for both intake and exhaust. Also included in this "engine on paper" is a good pair of pipes, and a high-quality aftermarket ignition system. A milder version of this same engine (one we didn't have room to include here) would differ by having a milder EV 46 camshaft - which doesn't need as much compression - so the heads would be shaved only .060 inches. (Some material found on the carts has been deleted, so they would fit on one page.)

```
FILE : COMB3

BORE DIA.        3.498                FLOW CORRECTION   11 CFM
STROKE LENGTH    4.250
ROD LENGTH       7.439                ROD/STROKE RATIO  1.75:1
NO. CYLINDERS    2
CUBIC INCH ---------------   81.69
COMBUSTION CHAMBER CC = 74.4  QUENCH CC =  0.0  TOTAL CC = 74.4
          COMPRESSION RATIO 10.0:1
                                        HEAD         PISTON VELOCITY
    *****CRANKSHAFT HORSEPOWER*****      C.F.M.      ¦***************¦
    R.P.M.     H.P.   PER CYL. PER C.I.  TORQUE   REQ.@10   VE     MAX      AVG.
    3000      51.91    25.95    0.6       90.9      72.7   104%  3472.22  2125.00
    3500      65.66    32.83    0.8       98.5      84.3   113%  4050.92  2479.17
    4000      76.91    38.45    0.9      101.0      96.0   116%  4629.62  2833.33
    4500      89.68    44.84    1.1      104.7     108.1   120%  5208.32  3187.50
    5000     102.04    51.02    1.2      107.2     121.9   123%  5787.03  3541.67
    5500     109.68    54.84    1.3      104.7     134.5   120%  6365.73  3895.83
    6000     115.06    57.53    1.4      100.7     146.3   116%  6944.43  4250.00
    6500     114.29    57.15    1.4       92.3     160.0   106%  7523.13  4604.17
    ----------------------------------------------------------------------------

             OPEN / CLOSE   DURATION    VALVE LIFT    LOBE CENTER   ROCKER RATIO
    INTAKE   18.0 / 50.0     248.0    NET.345  .560     106.0        1.625:1
    EXHAUST  54.0 / 18.0     252.0    NET.345  .560     108.0        1.625:1
                                       OVERLAP
             OVERLAP        [ PERCENTAGE ]         LOBE SEPARATION ANGLE
             36.0           [  6.3 % ]                   107.0

CAMSHAFT DESCRIPTION :
ACCELERATOR 560V (VIPER)    BIG-TWIN  HYD. OR SOLID LIFTER
                         (PERFORMANCE VALVE SPRINGS REQ.)

THE BEST CAM FOR HIGHER COMPRESSION 80 INCH  9:1-11:1 CR.
GOOD FOR STROKERS UP TO 96 CI. WANTING LOTS OF TORQUE.

PERCENTAGE OF CAMSHAFT OCCUPYING CYLINDER  116.7 PERCENT
110% TO 120%:MEDIUM PERCENTAGE.GOOD HIGH PERFORMANCE STREET, MID TO TOP END.

ESTIMATED STATIC COMPRESSION RANGE 154.6 PSI
145 TO 165 PSI:MODIFIED STREET MOTORS.DESIRABLE FOR H.P. STREET MOTORS.
-------------------------------------------------------------------------------
CYLINDER HEAD [CFM] FLOW CHART REQUIREMENTS TO OBTAIN ESTIMATED HORSEPOWER

     TOTAL          INT.          EXH.          INT.          EXH.
   VALVE LIFT     CFM @ 10      CFM @ 10      CFM @ 25      CFM @ 25
      .100          41.2          30.9          65.1          48.8
      .200          82.4          61.8         130.2          97.7
      .300         117.8          88.3         186.1         139.5
      .400         147.2         110.4         232.6         174.4
      .560         160.0         120.0         252.8         189.6

CARBURETOR FLOW REQUIREMENTS AT 10.0 INCH   153.2 C.F.M
```

Chart number 3: This engine is another 80 cubic inch V-Twin. Additional power is obtained through the use of ported S&S heads and (note the head CFM values are higher than in the last example) a 560 Viper camshaft from Power House - 242 and 246 are the duration figures for intake and exhaust with .560 inches of lift. This engine also benefits from a good after-market ignition including a high-performance coil, wires and module. Note, the cylinder head flow chart is calculated by the computer based on the single figure the operator puts in for intake flow at maximum valve lift. Also note, the program provides a minimum CFM that the carburetor must flow in order to achieve the horsepower and torque figures shown.

```
FILE : COMB4

BORE DIA.          3.625          FLOW CORRECTION   -5 CFM
STROKE LENGTH      4.625
ROD LENGTH         7.440          ROD/STROKE RATIO  1.61:1
NO. CYLINDERS      2
CUBIC INCH -------------- 95.47

COMBUSTION CHAMBER CC = 87.0  QUENCH CC =  0.0  TOTAL CC = 87.0
          COMPRESSION RATIO 10.0:1

                                          HEAD           PISTON VELOCITY
      *****CRANKSHAFT HORSEPOWER*****      C.F.M.      |****************|
   R.P.M.     H.P.   PER CYL. PER C.I. TORQUE  REQ.@10   VE    MAX      AVG.
    3000     55.13    27.56    0.6     96.5    79.9    91%  3805.57  2312.70
    3500     66.67    33.33    0.7    100.0    93.4    94%  4439.83  2698.15
    4000     79.63    39.81    0.8    104.5   106.9    98%  5074.09  3083.60
    4500     93.33    46.67    1.0    108.9   120.2   102%  5708.35  3469.05
    5000    113.51    56.76    1.2    119.2   132.8   112%  6342.62  3854.50
    5500    125.86    62.93    1.3    120.2   145.9   113%  6976.88  4239.95
    6000    132.47    66.23    1.4    116.0   159.4   109%  7611.14  4625.40
    6500    134.88    67.44    1.4    109.0   172.0   102%  8245.40  5010.85
  ----------------------------------------------------------------------------
              OPEN / CLOSE   DURATION   VALVE LIFT   LOBE CENTER  ROCKER RATIO
   INTAKE     24.0 / 60.0     264.0    NET.366  .595    108.0      1.625:1
   EXHAUST    64.0 / 20.0     264.0    NET.366  .595    112.0      1.625:1
                                       OVERLAP
              OVERLAP        [ PERCENTAGE ]        LOBE SEPARATION ANGLE
               44.0          [  9.5 % ]                  110.0

CAMSHAFT DESCRIPTION :
ACCELERATOR 595E (EXTREME) BIG-TWIN EVO ( HYD. OR SOLID )
                    (VALVE SPRING AND PORTED HEADS)

HOT SET-UP FOR 88-98 CI STREET STROKERS.
KILLER CAM FOR STREET STROKERS UP TO 103 CI, BELOW 10.5 CR.

PERCENTAGE OF CAMSHAFT OCCUPYING CYLINDER  124.7 PERCENT
120% TO 130%:HIGH PERCENTAGE HIGH PERFORMANCE STREET / STRIP.LIKES COMPRESSIO


ESTIMATED STATIC COMPRESSION RANGE 147.4 PSI
145 TO 165 PSI:MODIFIED STREET MOTORS.DESIRABLE FOR H.P. STREET MOTORS.

CYLINDER HEAD [CFM] FLOW CHART REQUIREMENTS TO OBTAIN ESTIMATED HORSEPOWER
     TOTAL        INT.        EXH.         INT.        EXH.
   VALVE LIFT   CFM @ 10    CFM @ 10    CFM @ 25    CFM @ 25
      .100        41.6        31.2        65.7        49.3
      .200        83.2        62.4       131.4        98.6
      .300       118.8        89.1       187.8       140.8
      .400       148.6       111.4       234.7       176.0
      .595       161.5       121.1       255.1       191.3
CARBURETOR FLOW REQUIREMENTS AT 10.0 INCH   187.7 C.F.M
```

Chart number 4. Now we're rockin'. This 96 cubic inch V-Twin should put a smile on the face of the most jaded rider. The extra cubes come from both a longer stroke and a larger bore diameter. The heads are from S&S, with mild porting to further increase their ability to flow large volumes of air. The camshaft is the same 560 Viper seen in the last example. With the increased cubic inches we see significant increases in both horsepower and torque.

In Lee's words, "This is a means of predicting the outcome, in terms of horsepower and torque, of various engine combinations." Is it accurate? Lee has been able to run some of his engines on the Custom Chrome dyno after building them with the help of the Walters software package and found the horsepower and torque to be almost exactly what was predicted by the computer allowing for a 15% difference between power measured at the crankshaft and that measured at the rear wheel.

As with any other tool the outcome or success of this software is dependent on the skill of the operator. When computers were new there was a popular phrase, "garbage in, garbage out." That pretty well sums up the idea that the computer can only process the information it is provided. The Walters software is no different. Though it's not terribly complex, it

> **As with any other tool the outcome or success of this software is dependent on the skill of the operator. When computers were new there was a popular phrase, "garbage in, garbage out."**

does work best in the right hands. Lee warns that you might, for example, plug in a combination of parts and see real big horsepower numbers, but you have to be savvy enough to look for horsepower and torque in the RPM range where the owner is likely to ride.

By inserting the CC volume, or a known compression ratio, the program will give you either a standard or corrected compression ratio (which takes into account the effect of the camshaft on the compression ratio the engine actually sees). The software also provides a static compression figure, a good indicator of starting troubles if it's too high.

An important input is that for the CFM (Cubic Feet per Minute) measurement that the heads will flow. In this way an engine builder can measure the exact effect of a good porting job on engine output.

In addition to predicting horsepower and torque

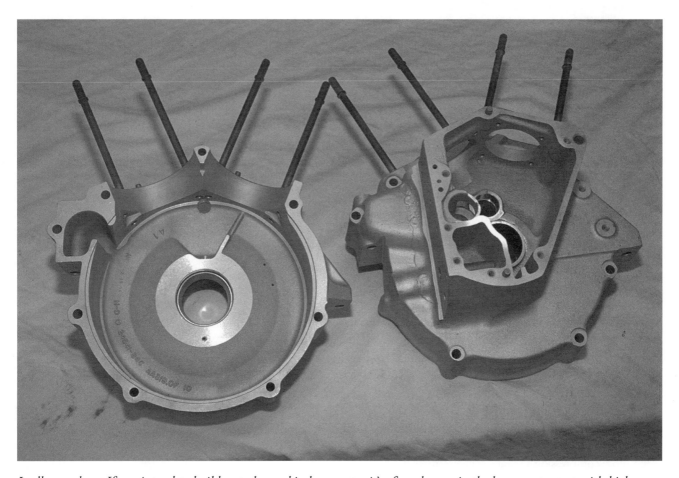

It all starts here. If you intend to build a stroker or big-bore motor it's often cheaper in the long run to start with high-quality aftermarket engine cases.

The flow bench in Lee Wickstrom's shop - an essential tool for anyone who does porting work. The vertical manometer on the left is how Lee calibrates the flow bench.

throughout the RPM range, the program gives a prediction of volumetric efficiency and also provides piston velocity. The piston velocity, given at both an average and maximum figure, is a good way to predict future troubles with stroker motors.

Some of the information is generated on the screen and is not part of the printout. Like the cam warning screen, which provides specific warnings if the cam choice is way off the mark. To illustrate this screen, Lee plugged in a stock Evo with stock compression and a relatively wild camshaft. The screen warned that the given combination would result in mid-range power that was "not adequate."

"This software package is a good way to gauge the potential of different combinations," explains Lee. "The biggest thing I learned is the relationship between the camshaft and the compression ratio. In most cases you need more compression to make that aftermarket camshaft work to its full potential."

This program will also predict E.T. times and trap speed at the drag strip, though Lee feels the real value of

the program is in its ability to test the ability of various engine packages. The Walters software is also a good tool for the Kokesh shop, a great way to show customers what they're likely to get from a particular part and in some cases convince them to use parts which are different than those they originally had in mind.

As an illustration of this software Lee put together three engine scenarios and ran them through the computer "dyno." There are actually two lessons to be learned from this illustration. One, what you can do with this new technology. Two, this is a good look at the performance of three logical engine combinations you might chose for your own bike. The three engines start with a modified 80 cubic inch factory motor and end with a strong running 96 cubic inch S&S engine. For more on these three engines see the reproduced printouts.

PORTING the V-Twin

The analogy is often made that an engine is nothing more than an air pump. If you want more power you've

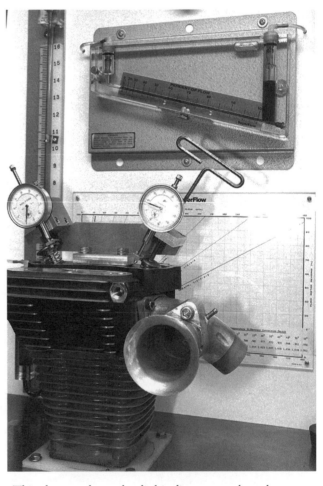

This close up shows the dial indicators on the valve stems and the second manometer - which gives a reading for percentage of flow, which converts to a CFM reading.

got to get more air in and out of that engine. Thus we add bigger carburetors, less restrictive exhaust pipes, and ported heads.

In most cases the biggest single restriction to flow is not the carburetor or the pipes but rather the passages through the head itself. "Porting", or reshaping the passages in the head, has become more and more common in recent years as riders and builders work to extract more and more power from the basic V-Twin design.

Porting is actually a bit of a misnomer because the area most in need of reshaping is not the port but the passage just behind the seat. Part science and part art, porting is best done in a shop with a flow bench to verify results. "I've seen heads where someone did a lot of work on the port itself," explains Lee. "When I put the heads on the flow bench they flow only the same as stock. I always figure people like that don't have the flow bench so they really don't know what works and what doesn't. And even some porting jobs that look good don't flow as much as you'd think. I think every porting job should come with a flow sheet so the owner knows what they've really got."

The flow bench is like a bare cylinder with a vacuum motor attached to the bottom side. With a cylinder head bolted to the top of the cylinder Lee is able to open each valve in small increments and measure the flow at each opening.

When you see the results from a flow bench you also see the specification that the head

Lee's porting tools, a small die-grinder and a series of stones and cutting tips.

While factory heads utilize a D-shaped combustion chamber, high performance castings tend to have a more oval combustion chamber shape and often feature twin spark plugs.

Lee at work in his home shop. The flow bench verifies the increased flow that comes about as the result of a good porting job - the computer and software are a good way to check the actual net effect of those increased CFM values on horsepower and torque.

The Harley-Davidson Complete Engine Program.

Sometimes called "crate" motors, Harley-Davidson dealers do sell complete engine assemblies. George Edwards from St. Paul Harley-Davidson explained that the Capitol Drive plant in Milwaukee produces a small surplus of engines and these are allocated to the dealers throughout the year based on the number of new motorcycles that each dealer sells.

George went on to explain that these are current production engines only. You cannot buy a complete Shovelhead engine, though you can probably still buy most of the parts from the dealer to build a complete 1973 and up Shovelhead, but I digress.

Each engine comes with an MSO, Manufacturer's Statement of Origin, which will make it easier to register your new bike when it's all finished. In terms of price you can probably have an engine built from aftermarket pieces for less than the total cost of the Harley-Davidson engine. But before discounting the possibility of using a genuine V-Twin, consider some of the advantages. "We offer a 90 day warranty, just like all the others," explains George. "But a lot of times that 90 day period starts on the date of purchase, so by the time the bike is assembled you don't really have very much warranty left. At St. Paul we offer a one year warranty from the date the bike is first started, *if the customer brings it here and lets us fire it for the first time.*" Other dealers have other policies. It's a good

We update Ultimate V-Twin Motorcycle as Harley-Davidson continues the transition from the Evo to the Twin-cam. Lance Kugler, new parts manager from St. Paul H-D, explains: "We only sell engines that are 'current production.' We have a good supply of Twin-cam engines available, along with Evos, but I don't know how long the Evos will be available. These crate engines are priced competitively with the aftermarket, and its hard to beat the reliability and parts availability of a H-D engine." Twin-cam engines come polished or in black and chrome, typically with no carb or intake. Complete fuel injected engines, and the counter-balanced Softail engines, are not currently available.

idea to check around before you commit to buying any engine."

"These are complete engines with the alternator, carburetor, and the ignition system minus the module. Each one has been run on a test stand at the factory and must pass all the items on their check list before it is shipped. The other thing people should remember is the fact that most dealers will discount the list price of those engines. This will depend on the dealer's situation of course, but it's worth asking about. I go a bit further, if the person buys the engine from us I offer a 20% discount on all the rest of the Harley-Davidson parts they buy to complete the project and 20% off on most aftermarket parts they buy at our store (a few aftermarket items don't have enough margin to offer the 20% discount)."

George went on to explain the engine you use may affect the cost of your insurance. "Buyers should be aware of insurance compa-

ny considerations before completing the bike. Some insurance companies classify scratch-built bikes as high performance bikes. You may want to check with your insurance company before choosing an engine to see if a genuine Harley-Davidson engine will change that classification. Something to consider before you make a final decision on where to buy your new motor.

George went on to explain that complete transmissions are also available from the local dealer. "As with the engine program, the complete transmissions are allocated to the dealers so availability may differ from one dealer to another. Genuine Harley transmissions are preferred by many because of a relatively new feature: HCR (high contact ratio) gears. These are much quieter and stronger then similar items from other companies."

Again, only current production transmission are available as a complete unit. You can't for example buy a complete FXR unit from a Harley-Davidson dealer (as the FXR is no longer in production). Some builders however, buy a complete current production transmission, then buy the genuine Harley-Davidson case and then put the factory gears in the factory FXR case.

In closing George added that the transmission cases from Milwaukee do not come with an MSO, so be sure the receipt you get lists the serial number on the case.

Like the engines, the five speed transmissions come complete. Offerings include all current production transmissions - available in limited numbers from your local dealer.

If you don't buy a complete transmission then consider buying a case and a separate gear set - both are available from either your dealer or the aftermarket.

flowed so many CFM at "ten inches of water." The "inches of water" is essentially a vacuum reading. To compare two flow readings they should both have been made at the same vacuum reading - or they can be converted through the use of a formula so the reading made at ten inches of water can be compared to that made at 20 inches of water.

Lee starts his porting jobs by doing a good three angle valve job. "I do the three-angle valve job, which defines the 45 degree seating area, and then radius the port from the inside of that seat area right down into the port itself," explains Lee. After doing nearly 200 porting jobs, Lee has a pretty good handle on what works and what doesn't. Most of the time Lee shaves the heads at the same time in order to increase the compression. That way the owner gets the full benefit of the camshaft that is often added at the same time the porting work is done.

Modifying a head is much like modifying an engine - at least in the sense that you get the biggest return early in the modification curve. Porting a head is a labor intensive operation. Lee explains that he does plenty of porting work on stock Harley-Davidson heads, but that, "It doesn't make sense to get real radical with those heads because by the time the customer pays me for all those hours he or she could go out and buy a different set of heads that flow more in their stock condition than the Harley heads do after they're ported."

In the end, porting the heads is just like the other engine modifications described here. It's a good way to add power to your V-Twin, but only if it's done in concert with all the other parts you put into that new engine.

TRANSMISSIONS

Virgins to this Big Twin motorcycle business might think that all five-speed transmissions are the same. Wrong. In current Harley-Davidson production there are three basic versions of the five-speed transmission - the Dyna model, the FL model and one more for Softail bikes. While the Softail transmissions bolt directly to the frame, the "rubber mount" (read Dyna, FXR and Dressers) suspend the engine and transmission in rubber mounts, one of which is located at the back of the transmission.

When it comes time to pick a transmission, you need first to pick the case style you require. The case is generally dictated by the frame manufacturer. Nearly all soft-tail style frames, for example, mount the transmission and engine directly to the frame and thus call for a soft-tail style transmission case.

When it comes to choosing a rubber-mount transmission case the Dyna, FXR and Dresser *cases* are all available from Harley-Davidson.

Delkron makes a new FXR case that is cast from 356 aluminum. This case will accept all standard five-speed gear

Displacing 80 cubic inches, this "shop project" V-Twin at the Kokesh shop features factory heads with oversize valves and a bathtub combustion chamber shape.

sets. Also, note that the Dyna and FL style cases use an oil tank mounted under the transmission which frees up that space that would otherwise be occupied by the oil tank.

Once you know which case style will work with your frame choice you can buy a case and fill it with the gear set of your choice, or buy a complete package. As noted in the side bar, Harley-Davidson dealers do sell complete five speed transmissions on a case by case basis (no pun intended). They also sell gear sets that can be fit into aftermarket cases. Complete gear sets, cut from high quality steel and back cut for easier shifting, are available from RevTech and Andrews.

When I asked George Edwards from St. Paul Harley-Davidson about transmission options he warned that they see a lot of customers who bought an engine, then a transmission and finally the inner primary that connects the two. "There are a number of different primary types out there," explained George. "The inner primary needs to be matched to the transmission you run."

The inner primary in turn will determine which starter you need. This is a case where it helps to buy the transmission, inner and outer primary, primary drive and starter assembly from one reputable shop that can provide the right stuff the first time.

INTERVIEW, CARL MORROW OF CARL'S SPEED SHOP

For a look at the possible use of some larger than 80 cubic inch V-Twins built by professional shops, I called Carl Morrow from Carl's Speed Shop. After thirty years in the business Carl understands the unique needs of a hot rod V-Twin. If 30

These back cut gear sets are available from RevTech in models to fit all five speed cases and applications.

Among the available engine options are these Power House engine kits available in displacements from 80 to 96 cubic inches. Mid-USA

years isn't enough, consider his many competition wins: including the Flash Race in Sturgis two years running (Fastest Legal All Street Harley, sponsored by American Iron magazine) and the Custom Chrome Dyno Shoot Out - which they won with an astonishing 228 horsepower from 98 cubic inches!

Carl, give me an example of a good V-Twin that a builder can buy as a complete unit without breaking the bank?

Well for between six and seven thousand dollars you can buy one of our complete engines without the polished cases. We build these from scratch, based on S&S cases, cylinders and pistons combined with stock Harley-Davidson flywheel assemblies. The stock four and a quarter inch stroke combined with a three and five-eighths inch diameter bore yields a total of 88 cubic inches. We use our CM 580 camshaft (.580 inches of lift and 246 degrees of duration on the intake and exhaust) with Harley-Davidson head castings that we port and assemble. With our Typhoon carburetor and True Flow exhaust these units will turn about 95 horsepower at the rear wheel, compared to about 52 horses for a stock V-Twin. It works out to be a nice smooth engine. It has the stock stroke so it will give good service and great reliability.

What if a builder wants more than that, what's the next logical step - and do people run into "diminishing returns" as they spend more and more money on the engine?

Well to go beyond our 95 horse unit it starts to get pretty expensive. Now you're approaching nine thousand dollars to buy a motor with 110 horsepower and tremendous torque. We increase the bore size again to 3-13/16 inches and retain the stock stroke. This nets out to 97 cubic inches. We use S&S cases and flywheels, and Axtell cylinders and pistons. The heads are STD castings that we port and assemble to our own specifications. The cam is a CM 612. Again, we like our own Typhoon carb and True Flow exhaust. We prefer to ship these as complete units with the carb and the pipes. That way all the

Here you see a factory clutch assembly - which can be upgraded by replacing the fiber discs with heavy duty Kevlar discs.

customer has to do is install the engine, we know it has the right jets in the carb and all the rest. Of course we can dress this up if you want with Arlen Ness goodies and all kinds of billet jewelry.

Obviously you prefer to get your extra cubic inches with a bigger bore as opposed to a longer stroke?

Yes, you avoid problems with high piston speed and damage to the primaries and reduced engine life.

Do these higher horsepower units require a transmission better than the factory five speed?

No, either of the engines I mentioned will work just fine with the stock H-D transmission, as long as you don't speed shift. By the way, we don't speed shift when we run on the drag strip.

What are the trade offs you make as you get up into the more powerful, more expensive units?

There are none at the 88 cubic inch level. None at the 97 either, The 97 might run a little hotter. But this is

> ## Either of the engines I mentioned will work just fine with the stock H-D transmission, as long as you don't speed shift.

a motor you could still use to run a lot of highway miles.

At what point in the modification curve does a person need to step up to better ignition?

You can use the stock ignition with a better module for awhile. But pretty soon (as you increase the horsepower) you need something like a Crane or Compu-fire ignition.

What about the relationship between compression and camshaft duration?

Well with more duration you need more compression because the valves are open longer. We like 8.9 to 1 compression, cranking. You have to use the correct cam with the right duration for the application. Head flow is very important, but so are all the parts.

What are the mistakes people make when they build high-performance engines?

They do sloppy work. Sometimes they use the wrong parts, wrong in the sense that the parts they use don't complement each other, and they forget the Pingel fuel tap.

For the ultimate in shine, some builders polish the fins and eliminate the bottom 3 fins completely.

Chapter Five

The Sheet Metal

Make it flow as well as go

The frame forms the foundation for the bike and the engine makes it go down the road. That doesn't mean the sheet metal isn't important. The tank(s) and fenders you hang on that bike will determine the look. As part of the planning process you must ask yourself if you're trying to duplicate an existing bike from Milwaukee or build a totally unique style of your own. The sheet metal (even if it's made of fiberglass) you chose and the way in which it is mounted on the bike is very important to the success of your

Complement the design of those flamed accessories with a flamed dash panel like this one. Drag Specialties

In just a few short years a number of new sheet metal designs have come on the market, including these aluminum tanks available from Pro One and others.

ting bigger. When you do the concept sketches for your new bike consider all the possibilities. Yes, you can have a fender made or modified to create a unique shape - but you don't have to.

MAKING THE SELECTIONS - GAS TANKS

Gas tank selection starts when you decide if the bike will be fat-bob or non-fat-bob style. Many frames, especially soft-tail style, come equipped with mounts for the two-piece fat-bob style tanks or offer that as an

project.

Up until a few years ago the number of fender and gas tank designs was rather limited. There were the standard OEM parts and replacements for those pieces and a few items like the Quick-Bob tanks for Sportsters. But if you wanted something "different" you really had to build it yourself. When asked, the major aftermarket manufacturers explained that they didn't offer more gas tank or fender designs because of the high cost of tooling.

In only a few short years we've gone from one extreme to the other. New designs for fenders and tanks appear on a regular basis in the New Products section of the popular magazines. No longer do you have to pick from only three gas-tank designs. Today we have beautiful, hand-formed aluminum tanks for sale from Arlen Ness, Pro One and many of the major catalog companies. And though they aren't cheap they're considerably less expensive than hiring your local metal-smith to make a similar tank from scratch.

Fenders now come in everything from small and bobbed to long and tail-dragging. These new designs are manufactured from fiberglass, ABS and even 18 gauge steel.

The range of sheet metal options is big and get-

It's the little things that count. Note how the elimination of the "oil tank bulge" really opens up the area under the seat on Rob Roehl's bike.

option on the "build sheet." With a frame thus equipped it's easy to mount a pair of three-and-a-half or five gallon tanks.

Builders should note that what we call "fat-bob" tanks come in two basic configurations: The solid-mount tanks used by the factory up to about 1984 and the rubber-mount (sometimes called "flat sided") tanks used from 1985 on. Most new frames come equipped for the late model rubber-mounted tanks.

If what you want is a fat-bob style tank but the two piece units seen like a lot of

Dave Perewitz talks about a "flow line" that gives his bikes their unique good looks. No matter how you define it, all the parts have to work together, or flow from one end to the other.

The shape of the gas tank(s) has a tremendous impact on the overall look of a motorcycle. Note how the extended tanks on this Perewitz bike arch over the rocker boxes.

work to mount, remember that one-piece fat-bob tanks are available with mounting kits from most of the catalog companies. Remember too that the two-piece tanks are available in at least three sizes or shapes, so pick the one that best matches the looks of the rest of the bike.

For those of you with stretched frames, "end caps" can be added to the stock tanks to stretch the silhouette. Pre-fab caps can be ordered from at least two aftermarket sources or fabricated by someone with good welding skills and access to some eighteen gauge steel.

A discussion of one-piece tanks must start with the FXR-style tanks. Many new frames are designed to accept a stock or slightly modified tank of this type, which is not to say that an aftermarket tank can't be used. For a stretched frame one of the new aluminum tanks would work very well, or you can have an existing tank extended by the fabricator of your choice.

MOUNTING THE TANK

Given the fact that V-Twin powered motorcycles vibrate, correctly mounting the tank to the bike so that it or the mounts don't crack is harder than it might seem. To quote Dave Perewitz, well-known builder of custom bikes, "At our shop when we mount a tank on a custom bike we always stay with the factory mounts or as close to the factory mounting system as we can. The point where the tank attaches to the bike needs to be really well supported, the factory does a nice job so we stay with their mounting system when we can."

If the frame you buy has no provision for mounting the fat-bob tanks, help is at hand. You don't have to fabricate your own mounting system because mounting kits for either early or late style tanks are available from most of the major aftermarket catalogs. These allow you to mount either style of tank to a frame with no mounts, or change from one style to the other.

Rob Roehl, who works for custom bike builder Donnie Smith of suburban Minneapolis, has the following observations about mounting tanks and fat-bob style tanks in particular.

"Most of the fat-bob style tanks we use now are the later versions, like these on this Kenny Boyce frame. They're all rubber mounted, not like the first ones that were solid mounted, you don't want to use those. These latest ones are really well supported, the mounting bosses are part of a big plate so there's a lot of support. Sometimes I cut off the front upper mounts and build a front mount that's down between the two tanks, that really cleans up the lines and gives me more options when it comes to making the dash.

"When people mount fat-bob style tanks they need to be sure the holes line up with the mounts on the frame. Sometimes they don't and then you have to heat and bend the mount so everything lines up. You can't mount these tanks with stress on the mounts or the mount will eventually crack.

"For one piece tanks where there is no mounting system I sometimes fabricate a mounting point below the center tube. Then I weld heavy tabs or brackets onto the bottom of the tank next to the tunnel that line up with the bracket that I've fabricated and welded to the center tube. I usually use a pair of mounting tabs at the front of the tank and another at the middle or the back. Sometimes you can't put the mounting tabs at the rear of the tank on the bottom because the tank sits so close to the rocker boxes that it's impossible to get at the bolts.

"If you're mounting a one-piece FXR-style tank, most mount solidly to the frame with attached brackets. Some aftermarket frames are designed for this type of gas tank but require that you change the rear

A variety of kits are available to mount both kinds of fat-bob tanks to frames without mounts - these are designed for the later rubber-mounted tanks. Drag Specialties

If you don't want to run fat-bob style tanks, some frames come equipped to mount a FXR tank. This KB frame uses the factory mounting at the front of the tank.

This is the rear of the same tank. Note, the factory mount has been cut off, replaced by neat little fabricated mounts underneath the tank.

73

Install a Flush-mount Gas Cap

Instead of looking for a "donor" tank to steal a gas cap assembly from, all you need is one of these assemblies from Custom Cycle Engineering.

Every body wants a neat Ninja-style gas cap these days, but the supply of Japanese donor tanks in the junk yards is dwindling. The answer to this shortage is a flush mount cap from Custom Cycle Engineering. By installing one of their assemblies you get a flush-mount gas cap without the hassle of buying an entire Japanese gas tank from the salvage yard.

All that's required is to cut a hole in the tank and weld in the base of the two-part cap assembly. Welding on gas tanks is never an easy task, so to see just how to do it right - without warping the top of the tank - I followed along as Rob Roehl from Donnie Smith's shop installed one of these cap assemblies in a modified after market tank. Rob explains the process, it's pretty straightforward and goes like this:

First Rob marks a centerline running the length of the tank. Next he finds the spot along the centerline where the cap looks the best. Then it's time to drill a pilot hole, and cut the hole for the base of the cap. The hole saw measures 2-3/4 inches in diameter, which is just lightly smaller than the O.D. of the cap assembly.

Rob uses a conventional hole saw from the hardware store, not a relatively expen-

A conventional hole-saw, just slightly smaller than the base for the new cap assembly, is used to cut the hole.

Here's the tank after the new hole is cut. Note the old caps, which were welded shut, and the extension on the end.

sive saw meant to cut metal. The saw works fine, though as Rob explains, "I don't spin the daylights out of it, as long as I keep the speed low it seems to work pretty well on metal."

Rob welds the cap in by first spot welding the lip in two places. Next he does four small stitches. All the welding is done with the heli-arc. Rob is always trying to keep the bead small and minimize heat build up. "If this were a Harley-Davidson tank I would be even more careful," explains Rob. "Because the metal on those is really thin, but this aftermarket tank is heavier so I don't have to worry quite so much about warpage and caving in the top of the tank"

After doing the 4 small beads Rob cools the tank with compressed air and takes a short break. Then it's time to do another series of beads followed by another cooling off period. Including the initial tack welds, Rob does the welding in four "installments" to avoid concentrating too much heat in the tank and having it warp. According to Rob, "The key is to take your time and allow the tank to cool off between welding sessions."

When Rob is all done, the tank has a nifty flush mount gas cap without the hassle of carving up another gas tank.

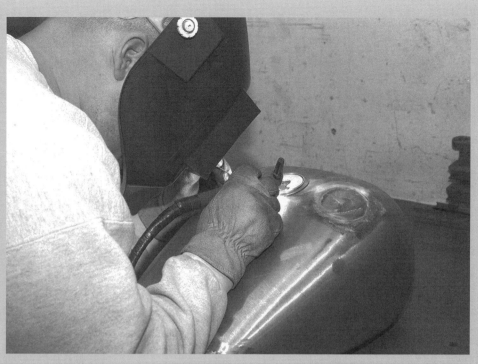

Rob welds in the base with the heli-arc welder to minimize warpage of the thin sheet metal.

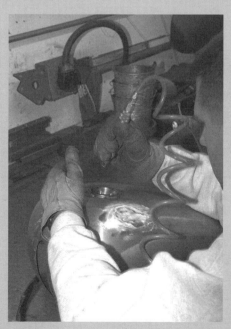

It's important to take a break between welding sessions. Here Rob uses compressed air to cool the top of the tank before doing more welding.

Nearly finished, note the welds are done in a series of small, even beads.

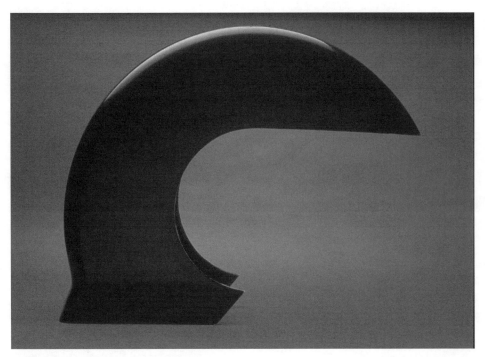

These Skirtdragger fenders are among the many designs in the Arlen Ness catalog. Arlen Ness Inc.

mounting bracket. If you go with one of the new custom tanks, then you will have to fabricate your own mounting system. Just be sure the tank is well supported and the mounting brackets are welded in place by a good welder to minimize stress on the tank and brittle welds and brackets.

MAKING THE SELECTIONS -
FENDERS

Choosing the fenders is more difficult than choosing a tank, simply because there are many more fender possibilities than there are tank choices. Jesse James, Arlen Ness, Paul Erpenbeck and Rick Doss are a few of the designers cranking out new fender designs available from Drag Specialties, Custom Chrome, Sumax and many more.

The fenders you choose need to match the design for the bike. There should be a certain harmony between the two fenders, the gas tank(s) and the lines of the bike. A nostalgia chopper-style bike needs an abbreviated front fender (or none at all) while a long sleek custom might look good with one of Arlen's cafe fenders. Anyone who puts on a lot of miles will want a slightly fuller front fender that does a good job of keeping the rain off the rider when you get caught in those occasional rain showers.

Some of the new fenders have exaggerated skirting on the side which makes it possible to buy the fender and then trim the skirting to suit your tastes. Which is probably easier for many of us than buying a fender and then welding on additional material to the side.

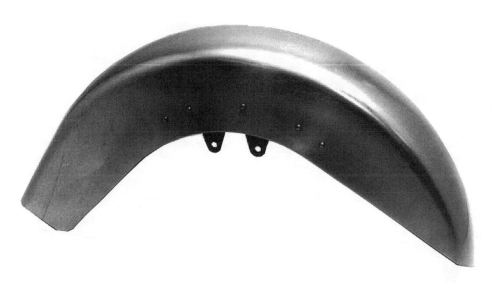

From the "always popular" department comes the classic shape of this Heritage style fender. Mid-USA

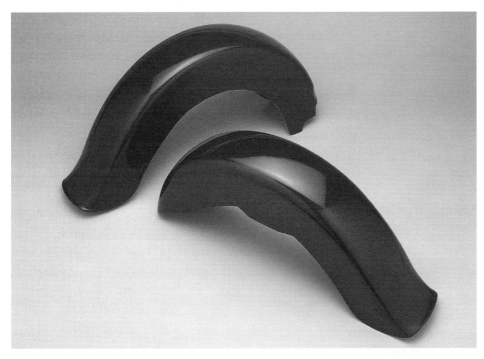

These fiberglass fenders from Bob McKay mimic factory shapes and come without holes so you can mount them exactly where you want. Custom Chrome

race tire might not grow much at all but a street tire usually will. When the fender is right down on top of the tire, or the brackets inside are real close to the tire, it might be fine at rest but at seventy or eighty miles per hour the tire will burn the paint off or expand enough to run into the edge of a bolt.

I always use button head bolts that screw up instead of down, so even if the tire does touch the bolt it isn't hitting a sharp edge that will tear the tire. People tend to ignore what might happen when the suspension bottoms hard.

Fiberglass designs make it very easy to trim the shape. In fact, some 'glass fenders require additional finishing before you can apply the primer and finish paint.

Choose carefully from among the vast number of fender designs. Find two that work well with each other and with the shape of the gas tank. These aren't just individual components you're bolting onto the bike, they are integral parts of the overall design.

MOUNTING THE FENDERS

If the bike you're building is a simple factory style bike with an OEM style chassis and sheet metal, then mounting the fenders is a relatively simple matter of bolting everything together. No matter how simple the bike is you need to be sure the fender fits the bike and that there is no chance it will hit the tire when the suspension bottoms.

You need to understand the suspension geometry to be absolutely sure the bolts for the fenders and struts don't come anywhere near the tire as the wheel moves over bumps.

If you're building a custom bike from a variety of aftermarket parts, then you need to consider the immortal words of fabricator Steve Davis, "When they mount fenders people need to remember that tires grow at speed and each tire is different. A road

Steve Laugtug's goal is a bolt-together bike with minimal fabrication (see Chapter 10). Both the front and rear fenders are from Jesse James.

77

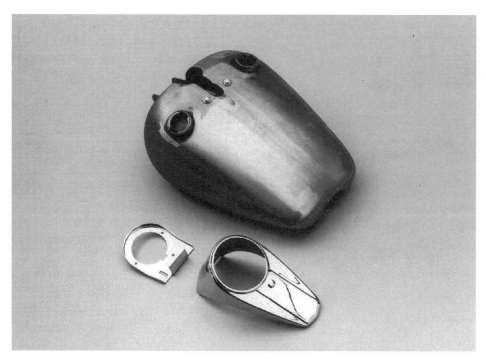

This quickbob tank with dash is intended for Sportsters, though similar designs are available for FXR-style chassis. Drag Specialties.

You need to know how the geometry works. If the fender looks OK when it's sitting but the tire moves through an unusual arc it might bottom or hit a bolt head when it bottoms - or hit the trailing edge of the fender (which will stop the tire dead). It sounds obvious, but people miss things like that all the time."

Like a gas tank, the fender you mount needs to be well supported. It's that old killer vibration again. Some builders hide extra support rails inside the fender, welded in place (or 'glassed in for a fiberglass fender). Self-locking ny-lock nuts are a good way to mount fiberglass parts because they "lock" without being so tight that you run the risk of cracking the fiberglass (many builders use these throughout the bike no matter what material the parts are made from).

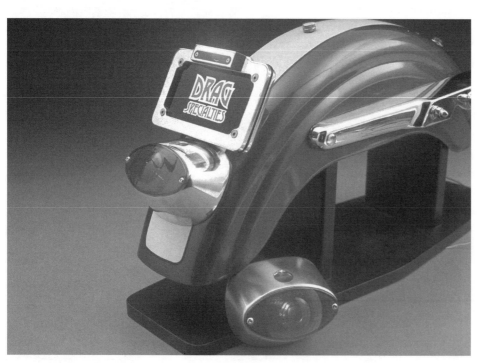

Show off your rear end with a FXR-style fender, billet license plate holder and "Hotop" taillight. Drag Specialties

The factory fenders often have little metal tabs inside to hold the wiring harness out of the way. Remember that when you add that wide rear tire, it's likely to run into those little tabs. At Minneapolis Custom Cycle, when they widen a fender they weld a small tube into the upper left corner for the wires to run through. No matter how big a bump you hit the tire will never reach up into the corner of the fender.

When you're mounting the fenders remember that just a small change in the position or angle of the fender has a tremendous impact on the way the whole bike looks. The inside radius of the fender needs to match and follow the diameter of the wheel and tire if possible. Spend time during the mock-up stage with the fender at different positions to see which one looks best.

DON'T FORGET THE MOCK-UP

All this business of making sure the fender is mounted correctly in a mechanical and aesthetic sense brings up the subject of the mock-up. Because you may not have built a bike before and because many of these "bolt together" projects really aren't, the mock-up stage is essential.

Get the bike up on a rack or sturdy bench so it's at a convenient height for you to work on. Now set the frame up at ride height if possible so you can accurately determine the clearance between the fender and tires and how the bike is really going to look when it's all assembled.

Getting it up off the floor makes it easier to stand back and get a good look at the bike so you can tell when something is out of proportion or just doesn't look right. If your shop is small put the bench on wheels so you can roll it outside and stand back far enough to really "see" the bike and make good judgments as to exactly where a fender or gas tank should mount.

The mock-up stage means you get to build this bike twice. During the mock up stage you should make sure everything fits and looks good. It's better to find out that the fender won't fit before you've gone to the trouble of painting it. If your fenders come without mounting holes (as many do) you need to determine not only *if* they will fit but also *where* they should sit.

If you're looking for a way to eliminate the big factory lights signals without having to use hand signals, consider these nifty fender struts with integral lights. Arlen Ness Inc.

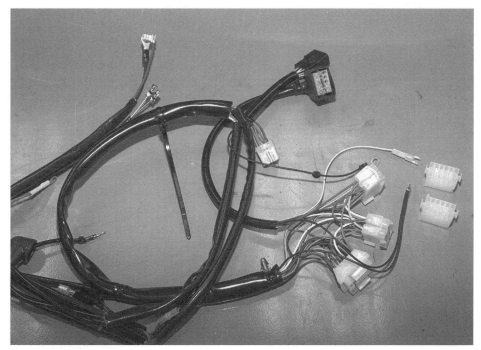

Most builders use a factory harness on their scratch-built bikes. With fat-bob tanks the Softail harness generally works best. If you've never wired a bike before, don't be afraid to ask for help.

Many frames have the correct holes in the webbing below the top tube so the plugs on the factory harness will snap right in.

You can buy harness plugs, which match the plugs in the factory harness, from any good motorcycle parts outlet (see Chapter 8 and 9 for more on wiring).

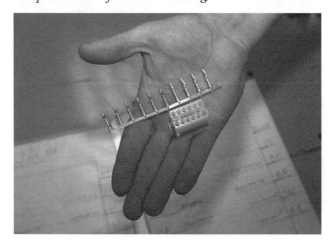

Here you can see the small pin connectors that snap into the harness plugs. Be sure to put the pins into the right spot because once they're in it's tough to get them out.

You started the project by making a sketch or altering a photograph. The mock-up stage is the time to decide if the choices you made were the right ones. Set the frame at ride height, install the motor, set the tank(s) in place and use clamps to hold the fenders on the bike. If the rear fender doesn't seem like the right piece beg, borrow or buy another. Clamp it in place and see which one you like better, which of the two better fits the character of the bike.

This is the time to make sure that all the bolt holes line up, that your choice of engine, transmission, and rear wheel will line up, and allow clearance for the belt or chain. Though this seems like extra work doing a mock-up saves time in the long run.

After you're happy with the look and fit of all the parts you can send everything out for painting and plating. When all those parts come back you can begin the assembly with the confidence that all the parts are the right ones for the bike and that each one will fit without having to enlarge the holes or relocate the fender.

WIRING

The wiring harness you use is determined primarily by the frame. A harness for a Softail (available from the dealer) works best if the bike has fat-bob style tanks with the dash between the tanks. If you intend to use a one piece gas tank and put the ignition switch down on the left side then a harness for an FXR might work better. If you're in doubt about which is the right harness ask the frame manufacturer or dealer for a recommendation.

Though it might be tempting to just make up your own harness and eliminate all those "extra' wires it's not a good idea, unless you're an experienced mechanic with a good handle on wiring and D.C. electricity. Consider the basic needs for ignition, starting and turn signals. Even more important is the fact that the harness you install should work without a glitch for the life of the vehicle.

Even with the factory harness there will be some additional hand-work the builder needs to do. The harnesses for each side of the bars for example must be trimmed to the correct length before each wire is crimped onto a small pin and the pin is inserted into a terminal block. Each pin must slide into the correct position in the terminal block, then the block can be connected to the matching block in the wiring harness.

You will need a manual with a good wiring dia-

ic. As for the wiring you do yourself just remember one thing: be neat, neat, neat. Use tape and tie-wraps to wrap wires into bundles and then into a harness. Don't let wires lie about loose. The fine print at the bottom of Murphy's law states that any loose wire that can possibly get pinched between the tank and frame (and cause weird intermittent electrical maladies) definitely will. So don't let it hang, make sure it's neatly wrapped into the harness with all the others.

The dash base includes 3, 15 amp circuit breakers, the ignition switch and assorted lights, all of which must be combined into a harness.

gram to determine where each wire goes in the terminal blocks and other details. (for more on wiring, see the assembly sequences in Chapters Eight and Nine). During the mock-up stage it's a good idea to figure out where you want things like the ignition module, ignition switch and horn. If you want them someplace other than the factory location, you will have to make modifications to the harness to get them there. 1991 and later wiring harnesses are set up to run a self-canceling module for the turn signals, though if the bulbs are of a different amperage draw than the stock units a Badlands unit will also need to be used to make the self-canceling module work correctly. And if you want to run front blinkers integrated into the mirrors (Whiskers) you will need to run one extra wire through the harness on either side of the bars.

When you do lengthen a wire so it will reach to the new location for the horn, be sure you use factory color codes and wire sizes. This will make the modified harness easier to trouble shoot later. Any wire you cut should be soldered back together and then sealed with a piece of shrink wrap. Don't use crimp connectors, especially in locations where they're sure to get wet, like under the fenders.

Remember that if you've never wired a bike before it might be better to take it to a good mechan-

There's nothing worse than a wiring harness with 15 red wires! Buy enough wire varieties that you can match the factory colors and sizes.

Paint Preparation

You might not want to do your own paint job, but it is often necessary to put some paint on all those bare metal parts in the garage simply so they won't pick up a layer of surface rust between the time you bring them home and the time the bike goes out for paint.

What follows is a quick look at primers. If you're going to shoot a quick coat of primer on the parts it might just as well be the right stuff, something that will make a good base under the finish paint.

Primer isn't just "primer." Primer comes in lacquer and two-part (often known as epoxy primer), as a sealer and as a primer-surfacer.

WAX AND GREASE REMOVERS

Wax and grease remover isn't even a paint, yet it is the first thing you should use on the surface before applying any kind of paint. If it ain't clean the paint won't stick - period.

METAL PREP

It's often a good idea to use a metal etch before spraying the first coat of primer. The metal etch prepares the bare metal for that first coat of paint. Though many shops spray epoxy primer over bare steel, many paint manufacturers recommend you treat the steel with metal etch first. Think of this as a primer for the primer.

PRIMER

A true primer is a paint material chosen for its good adhesion to the material it is sprayed over. Most provide good resistance to corrosion and moisture. A true primer is not meant to be sanded and contains a low percentage of solids.

PRIMER-SURFACER

Primer-surfacers are primer materials with a high solids content. While offering good adhesion like a straight primer, a primer-surfacer will help fill small scratches and imperfections, and sands easily. Primer-surfacers should be applied in two or three coats and then sanded when dry. If you fail to allow the material to dry properly before sanding it will shrink *after* you've finished sanding, allowing small scratches (known as sand scratches) to show through the finish paint job.

EPOXY PRIMER

An epoxy (or two-part) primer like DP 40 from PPG or KP-2 and EP-2 from House of Kolor is more durable, expensive primer material. These materials are known for their superior bonding abilities and great corrosion resistance. An epoxy primer is a good choice for motor-

Some two-part products, like this EP-2 from House of Kolor, can be used as both a pure primer and as a primer-surfacer. House of Kolor.

cycle gas tanks, and will help prevent spilled gasoline from working under the top coat of paint and causing a blister around the fill cap. (Note: always mask off the area where the gas cap seals, so the flexible seal in the gas cap rests against bare metal, not paint. This will help prevent the gas and fumes from working under the paint and causing a blister.)

The catalyst in these paints (at least in the case of PPG and House of Kolor's products) is not an isocyanate, (a highly toxic material often contained in paint catalysts) most painters spray these materials with only a charcoal type respirator. It should be noted that PPG recommends a fresh air hood in spite of the fact that there are no isocyanates in these products.

Some of these like the EP-2 and KP-2 from House of Kolor can be sanded like a primer-surfacer, while others are meant to be used as a strict primer. Many of these can be used as the sealer coat before the color coats are applied. Though they are durable and useful materials, each is a lit-

tle different so be sure to check the manufacturer's recommendations.

PRIMER-SEALER

A primer-sealer, sometimes known as a sealer, is meant to seal or separate two different layers of paint. A coat of sealer is often applied before starting with the first of the finish coats. This is not a sandable finish, but is meant to seal two different types of paint and to prevent the finish paint from soaking into the primer coats underneath.

WHAT ABOUT FIBERGLASS

What about primer for fiberglass fenders you say? Fiberglass parts can be painted with a good two-part primer, but you need to wash and scuff the parts first. To quote Jon Kosmoski, owner of House of Kolor, "The very first thing you need to know is that most of the companies that manufacture fiberglass parts use a water-borne mold-release agent. So the very first thing you want to do with those new parts is scrub them with hot soapy water and a scrub brush. You can use every solvent known to man and it will not take off the release agents, but soap and water will. If you sand it before you do this there's a good chance that you will grind this wax-like material into the surface of the gel-coat."

"Once you have washed the body use a solvent wash, and then take the DA sander with 80 grit and scratch the gel-coat thoroughly. You want to knock off all of the shine prior to application of the primer. I like to see people use our EP-2 two-part primer on the fiberglass. It takes a longer cure time, but believe me when I tell you that it will add years and years to the life of the paint job.

This K-36 primer-surfacer from PPG is designed to quickly fill small scratches and low spots, and sand easily.

Finish Paint

WHAT'S INSIDE THE PAINT CAN

Whether you mix and squirt the final paint yourself or pay the full-time professional at the paint shop you're going to need to understand the differences between urethane and lacquer. And before discussing the differences we first need to discuss the things that all paints have in common.

Any paint is made up of three basic components: pigment, resin and solvent, with a few additives.

Pigment is the material that gives the paint is color. Resin (also known as Binder) helps to hold the pigments together and keep them sticking to the metal. Solvent is the carrier used to make the paint thin enough to spray. In the case of lacquers a true thinner is used while in the case of an enamel the solvent is a reducer. Additives are materials added to the paint to give it a certain property or help it overcome a problem.

There are a few more terms to get out of the way. One that crops up is VOCs, or Volatile Organic Compounds. Another related term is Solids, as in, "high-solids" paint.

Going back to the three basic components of paint, the solvent (a volatile material) evaporates (or oxidizes) after the paint is sprayed on the bike leaving behind the pigment

Kandy colors are actually a tinted clear that you can see through. These from House of Kolor are a urethane material and must be clearcoated with a urethane clear.

and binder, known as the solids. Solvents that evaporate into the atmosphere are known in the industry as VOCs and have come under government regulation.

Paint manufacturers are trying to increase the percentage of solids in their paints in order to reduce the amount of solvent and thus the VOC emissions. In the case of sandable primers, the high-solids term means that the primer contains a high percentage of solids and that these solids will fill scratches and small imperfections in the surface.

THE THREE MAJOR TYPES OF PAINT

Most of the paints available for painting your motorcycle can be classified as either a lacquer, an enamel or a urethane. Though urethanes are technically an enamel, they will be considered as a separate type of paint.

ENAMEL

Most modern enamels are acrylic enamels (meaning they contain plastic), offering good flexibility and durability. Many modern enamel paints can be catalyzed with isocyanate, which aids cross-linking of the paint molecules thus improving the durability of the finish.

Enamel uses a reducer instead of a thinner, as the solvent part of the mix. An enamel paint job hardens as the reducer evaporates and the resin oxidizes (mixes with oxygen). The need for oxidation adds considerably to the drying time of an enamel paint job. Though there's nothing wrong with enamel paint, the vast majority of what we call "custom" paints are available as either a urethane or an acrylic lacquer.

LACQUER

Lacquer paints have been available for years. During the early 1950s, most of the custom cars and bikes were painted with lacquer, nitrocellulose lacquer to be exact. By the late 1950s everyone had switched to a new lacquer formula - acrylic lacquer. This new material provided better resistance to ultraviolet radiation and also gave the paint more flexibility.

Custom painters have always liked lacquer because of it's fast drying times, great color and the ease with which spot repairs can be made. Painters often put lacquer on in multiple coats, wet sanding between coats. The end result is that deep shine you can almost swim in.

The trouble with acrylic lacquer is it's lack of durability and the maintenance a lacquer paint job requires. The great lacquer shine comes only after plenty of wet sanding and polishing. The other problem with lacquer paints is the VOC issue discussed earlier. The evaporating thinner and the multiple coats (more thinner) means that spraying lacquer puts a relatively large amount of VOCs in the atmosphere.

URETHANE

The hot stuff in the custom painting field is urethane. Technically, urethane is an enamel, yet it sprays much like a lacquer. Urethane is a relatively new two-part paint material catalyzed with isocyanate. Even though it's classed as an enamel, urethane dries very fast and offers easy spot repairs. The fast drying means quick application of second coats, easy candy paint jobs and fast tape outs for flame jobs and graphics. Urethane is super durable, resisting rock chips and chemical stains better than anything except powder coating.

The biggest downside to the urethane paints is the toxicity of the catalyst, the isocyanates. These materials are so toxic that spraying with urethanes requires a fresh-air system (especially in the home painting situation where ventilation is limited) so the painter is sure to breathe absolutely no shop air. The other downside to urethanes is their higher cost.

So if you decide to "do it yourself" be sure you understand how to correctly use the paint materials. For lacquer, use a charcoal type respirator and for urethane, borrow or rent a fresh-air hood with a separate compressor. And ask for the Technical Information sheets on any paint you buy, they're a great source of information on mixing and application of the paint - and they're free.

Acrylic lacquers are still available from a variety of companies. Less toxic than urethanes, they are also less durable.

Chapter Six

Finance, Register and Insure

The Most Important Work Comes Last

THE PAPER WORK

They say the job isn't done until you've finished the paper work and building a bike is no different. Before buying all those expensive parts you probably need to borrow some money. And before taking that first big ride you're going to have to register and insure the new beast. What follows are some ideas and insights intended to help you wade through the financial and regulatory road blocks.

WHERE TO GET THE BUCKS

If you've got the money to build that bike already in the bank, then more power to you. For

Insuring your scratch-built bike will probably mean sending photos to the insurance company or agent and having the bike appraised for a true value.

*Sooner or later it happens to all of us. And when it does you
want your paper work and registration squeaky clean!*

MANUFACTURER'S CERTIFICATE OF ORIGIN
-- MOTORCYCLE FRAMES --

The undersigned MANUFACTURER hereby certifies that the new Motorcycle Frame described below, is the property of said MANUFACTURER, and is transferred this

twelfth _____ day of August _____ 19 94

on Invoice No. 03293 _____

to _____
DISTRIBUTOR, DEALER, ETC.

whose address is _____
STREET

_____ _____
CITY   PROV.

Shipping Weight 63 _____ Length in Inches _____

Type of Frame 520-4 FXST _____

Serial # 2T91FDL24RR097837 _____

The MANUFACTURER certifies the above statements are true and correct and that this was the first transfer of such new motorcycle frame in ordinary trade and commerce.

Executed on August 12, 1994 _____
DATE

at _____ RED DEER, ALBERTA _____
CITY   PROV.

Name of Manufacturer TRIPOLI MANUFACTURING

Signature of Company Official _W Lian_
SIGNATURE

Position or Title Shipping Officer

Manufacturer's Address (street) BOX 45, SITE 14, R.R. 1

City RED DEER Prov. ALBERTA

Postal Code T4N 5E1 Telephone Number (403) 347-8810

Both frames and engine cases come with a MSO, which must be properly filler out to obtain a legal registration. Each time the part changes hands, the transfer must be recorded on the MSO or an attached "assignment" sheet.

most of us however, the money will have to come from another source and most often that source is the local bank or credit union.

Borrowing money to buy a new factory bike is one thing. Finding the cash to buy a bike that really doesn't exist yet is much more difficult. Bankers tend to be conservative. Asking for a loan against something that may only exist in your mind is asking a lot. Financing a scratch-built bike *that's already assembled* isn't as tough, simply because the loan officer can see what it is and easily have it appraised. In these situations the bank or credit union can compare the assembled bike to those from Milwaukee when trying to establish the value.

Convincing your banker to borrow you the money to buy a pile of parts is a tough sell. As Greg Isaacson from Security State Bank in Marine on St. Croix, Minnesota, stated, "I'm going to look at who the person is rather than the value of the collateral. In a worst case situation if the bike is completely assembled and the borrower defaults on the note, we can sell it and probably turn out OK. But if we have to go collect the parts, and then sell those we're probably going to loose money."

It helps to have a good relationship with a bank or credit union, because as Greg says, they're really looking at you and not at the bike. If you don't have a long credit history with the local bank, look for a loan officer with a knowledge of motorcycles, as he or she might better understand what you're trying to do.

If you own your home long enough to build some equity, then there's another very attractive option. "The smart way to do is to borrow the money against your house," explains Greg. "Because generally the interest is tax deductible and you can do whatever you want to with the money."

The home equity loan is in fact how many of the buyers at stores like Minneapolis Custom Cycle and M-C Specialties are financing their new bikes. Some professional builders however, borrow money against the bike, identifying it only by the VIN number (essentially the frame number). In this way it's not so obvious that the bike may not be finished yet.

In the end you need good credit history and an understanding loan officer. The other option is to own a large piece of collateral (like your house) that doesn't already have a loan against the full value. Without one or the other it's going to be tough to borrow the money for your new Ultimate V-Twin.

REGISTER THAT NEW RIDE

One of the questions that comes up again and again is the potential hassles of registering one of these scratch built bikes. Rob Carlson from Kokesh Motorcycle Accessories outside of Minneapolis, Minnesota, has done it a number of times and describes the various steps he goes through (this is for Minnesota).

1. You must have a Manufacturer's Statement of Origin (known as the MSO) with serial numbers for the frame and engine cases. In the case of the transmission, Delkron supplies an MSO with the transmission, while Harley-Davidson only gives you a receipt with the serial number of the case.

2. You need *all* your receipts, the state wants to know that the parts are purchased and not stolen.

3. You must have the bike inspected at a DMV testing station. The bike must meet all current requirements for lights, turn signals, horn, and all the rest in effect as of the year it is being registered.

4. Rob always brings a cover letter explaining the bike and a list of all the parts with their price and the amount of state sales tax that has already been paid on the parts - so no sales tax is due on the bike or the parts.

5. Each state is different. Most require an inspection, though some focus on safety, and others want to be sure the parts are purchased and not stolen. Be sure to check the requirements for the state where you live.

Mike from M-C Specialties adds the following fine points:

"Keep a complete duplicate file of all receipts and paper work, because the state always looses

the file. Make sure you've got an MSO or receipt with a serial number for the transmission. Have as many receipts as possible. In Minnesota you have to fill out a Affidavit of Reconstruction (like you would for a bike that was "totaled" and rebuilt).

"In Minnesota, after they inspect the bike they give you a pass or fail on the form they fill out. Then you take that form to get the license plate. Usually you apply for title when you apply for the license plate but the process seems to change from year to year. I've learned to try and get all my ducks lined up before I get there so I don't look like a fool. They like to try and intimidate me, it helps to have all my paper work in order before I arrive. They give me a hard time for things like not being able to read the serial number on the transmission cases, because the cases were painted for example. Sometimes they want to see receipts for every nut, bolt and cotter key. Wisconsin is easier, any state trooper can do the inspection and then you just do down and get the plates."

For a look at the typical registration headaches in one more state I called Arlen Ness in California. Arlen in turn referred me to Lynrd, his resident registration expert.

Registration according to Lynrd requires two trips to the DMV and one to the California Highway Patrol. When you make your first trip to the DMV you need an Application for Original Registration form number 343. On this form you will list the make as: Special Construction and the year as "00." You will also need the MSO for the frame and engine. The MSOs must be filled out correctly and reflect each change in ownership. That is, if the frame passed through the hands of two shops before you bought it, those transfers must be noted.

You are not required to provide an MSO for the transmission, though there is a space for that on the application form. In California the MSOs do not have to be notarized.

You also need a Statement of Construction form number 105. This is where you set the value of the bike (which determines the cost of registration). Lynrd notes that sales tax is charged on all parts unless you can prove with receipts that the

tax has already been paid, or they are "parts of your own manufacture or parts from another motorcycle." You need receipts for everything you've purchased and though it's not required, Lynrd always includes a federal form number 236, for the odometer reading.

You also need a Brake and Light inspection, though it's tough because there are no certified brake and light inspectors in the state. Lynrd complies with the law by providing a number 256, Statement of Fact form, which must be filled out by a motorcycle service facility.

And we're not through yet. With all the above forms in hand and all the receipts, you make your way to the DMV, where they look everything over and give you a form number 124, which you in turn take to the Highway Patrol. They look over the bike and fill out the rest of the 124, which you then take back to the DMV so you can now get license plates and eventually the title.

Lynrd notes a few things he's learned along the way, "If it's an old frame with no numbers, the Highway patrol can issue the numbers when you go to them with the form 124. And by paying a fifteen dollar fee you can have them rush process the title so you get it back in only 72 hours. And always call for an appointment at the DMV, don't

go stand in line. You also need an appointment for the CHP, be sure the Vehicle Verification Officer will be there because that's who needs to make the inspection."

INSURANCE, THE NECESSARY EVIL

Insuring a scratch-built bike is kind of like financing one - it really helps if you've got a friend in the business. Some agents I spoke with said it was tough at best to insure a "custom bike." Other agents, those that work with the local shops who are building the bikes, seem to write insurance for these bikes just like they would for a new Harley-Davidson or Honda.

You need an agent who has some understanding of motorcycles or has some other reason to write insurance for your new bike. If you have the house, car and business insured with one agent, then he or she has an incentive to find a program to fit your new bike. Failing that, you may need to shop until you find an agent who writes motorcycle insurance and understands your new machine.

In almost any case you will need to provide photos of the bike and proof of title. Some states (like Minnesota) title the bikes like a re-constructed vehicle which raises red flags for the insurance companies. Doug Morgan, owner of Morgan's Number One Insurance in Minneapolis, has been insuring motorcycles for sixteen years. He explains that,

"Insurance companies work on the law of large numbers. If they insure a million Chevy Cavaliers, they know who drives those cars, what they're worth and what the average losses are over a given period. With these custom bikes, the numbers are so small they have no data and that makes the companies real nervous."

"Some of our companies will write a bike like this but there's a fifty percent surcharge. We've tried to help the insurance companies put together a program that's less expensive but so far they just don't want the business. If you tell the company (or agent) what it is and tell them that it's a 96 inch motor, then they may not want to write it at all. And if you lie on the application they can deny coverage if there's a loss. Sometimes I tell people to just buy liability coverage, keep the insurance costs down that way and accept the risk."

Even after you've found an agent who will write the policy you still need to establish a value. Some agencies simply use the value of a similar bike from Milwaukee. If your new machine is worth more than that you may need to buy an endorsement for the "extra" value and coverage. You may need to have a formal appraisal done by a local shop.

Patrick O'Phelan from O'Phelan Insurance in St. Paul, Minnesota, explains that the companies he works with, "don't like choppers built in the back yard, or a bike that's been heavily altered in any way. They often require a photo of the bike and if it's a stock looking bike you're usually OK. Some companies won't insure it unless it's a Harley-Davidson, so in those cases you may have to go find another agent and/or company."

Most insurance companies like it simple, a square peg in a square hole. Massaging a round peg to fit that same square hole is sometimes too difficult. As Patrick says, "You need an agent who knows the difference between one bike and another. One who understands what you have."

Mold, modify and customize the frame all you want. But make sure than when it comes time to register the beast, that the inspecting officer can still read the VIN or serial number usually found on the neck.

Chapter Seven

A Customized Soft-tail

From The Shop of Donnie Smith

A FOUNDER'S BIKE

At Donnie Smith's suburban Minneapolis shop, each of the big projects has a design goal. In the case of the soft-tail style bike seen here, the goal was to combine the new Donnie-Smith designed Chrome Specialties chassis with the limited-production 110 cubic inch engine from S&S. Both companies are celebrating significant birthdays, thus the bike became a "founder's bike" built to highlight the founding of both companies.

Built by Donnie Smith and crew to highlight the founding of both S&S and Chrome Specialties, this custom uses a Donnie Smith designed frame and limited production 110 inch S&S four-inch bore engine.

THE MAJOR COMPONENTS

Perhaps the most important of all the parts used to build a custom motorcycle is the frame. The look, style and handling are all determined by the series of tubes that connect the neck with the rear wheel.

The frame for this particular project is a special soft-tail style frame designed by Donnie for CSI. Though the frame uses typical soft-tail type geometry with the shocks placed under the transmission, this is one chassis that can hardly be called a standard aftermarket soft-tail. By moving the pivot for the swingarm inboard, Donnie's creation allows for plenty of belt clearance, even with a 180 or 200 series tire. Moving everything inboard has another advantage as well. The pivot and the support plates on this frame seem to disappear. This disappearance, combined with the unique swingarm, makes this chassis a much more convincing "hardtail."

The example seen here uses five inches of stretch and a thirty eight degree fork angle to give the bike what Donnie Smith calls an "attitude," and a good basis for some very nice lines.

A FOUR-INCH BORE

The engine in this ride is nearly as unique as the frame. The four-inch bore engines from S&S have become hugely popular. A good case of having your cake and eating it too, these engines provide enormous amounts of torque without the need for high compression pistons or radical camshafts. At S&S, the four-inch bore is commonly matched up to a crank assembly with four, four and a quarter or four and a half, inches of stroke. The resulting displacement nets out to 101, 107 or 113 cubic inches. For these special limited-edition V-Twins, S&S combined the popular four inch bore cylinders with a special flywheel assembly with a stroke of four and three-eighths inch for a total of 110 cubic inches of rumblin' V-twin.

THE ASSEMBLY BEGINS

John Galvin is the man in charge of the assem-

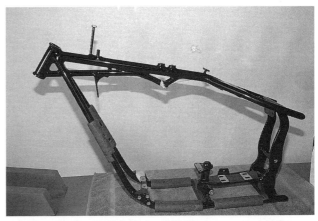

This particular model of the CSI frame came with five inches of stretch and a thirty-eight degree fork angle. Note how the areas where the engine and transmission mount were masked off to ensure a good solid connection.

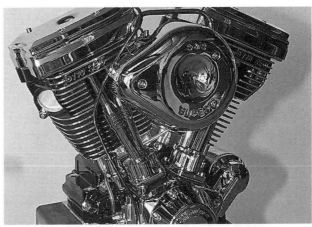

This 110 cubic inch S&S engine breathes through a Super G carburetor with help from a S&S camshaft. Donnie purchased the motor in pieces, so it could be carefully painted and polished before assembly.

Rob Roehl and Don Tima (far side) help with the engine installation. Note how the frame tubes are protected by foam and tape during the installation process.

With the engine in place it's time to set the transmission on the frame. Note the missing center tube in this Donnie-Smith designed frame.

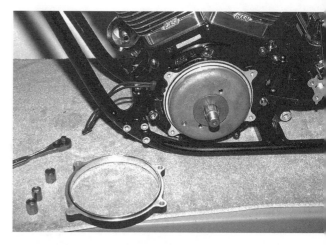

Because the transmission is off-set to the left in the frame you must use a spacer like this between the engine and the inner primary.

The transmission John sets in place is a complete five-speed assembly from CSI.

With the engine and transmission bolted in place (but not final tightened) it's time for the first fitting of the inner primary.

Now the engine and transmission mounting bolts can be slipped into place, though final tightening happens later.

An O-ring must be used between the engine and the spacer, and again between the spacer and the inner primary.

bly of this special V-twin. The photo sequence starts at the beginning of the final assembly sequence. This bike has already been assembled or mocked-up once, what we see here is the second or final assembly. As explained earlier in the book, it's important to build the bike twice. During the mock-up stage Donnie and the crew made sure that all the parts fit together, and that the finished bike has the look and the lines they were trying to achieve. The final assembly is just that, an assembly without the need to adjust any fender positions or weld last-minute tabs on the frame.

John starts with the painted frame, minus swingarm, sitting on the work surface. It's important to note that no paint was applied to the parts of the frame where the engine and tranny mount. In this way there is sure to be a good mechanical and electrical connection between engine and frame. Once John's shop-mates, Rob Roehl and Don Tima, help in setting the engine in place he uses a tapered punch to line up the engine mounting holes with those in the frame and then drops in the engine mounting bolts.

Next comes the five-speed transmission, delivered as a complete unit from CSI. John leaves both the engine and transmission mounting bolts snug, before installing the inner primary for the first time. Once he has the inner primary, and the spacer that moves the transmission over 1/2 inch to the left, bolted tightly to both the engine and the transmission, John can tighten the bolts holding both the engine and the transmission to the frame. Now it's time to take out the bolts holding the inner primary cover in place and check to make sure the inner primary will easily slide on and off the engine and transmission.

John's elaborate engine/transmission/inner primary installation procedure will ensure that the engine and transmission are correctly lined up. Part of this installation procedure is the red Loctite John uses on the engine and transmission mounting bolts.

Before the inner primary is bolted on for the last time, John slips the final drive belt in place.

The inner primary is installed for the first time only after the engine and transmission are snugged down to the frame.

After making sure the inner primary slides on and off, John puts the drive belt in place and mounts the inner primary for the last time.

Any bolt that isn't contained by lock tabs gets a shot of red Loctite before installation.

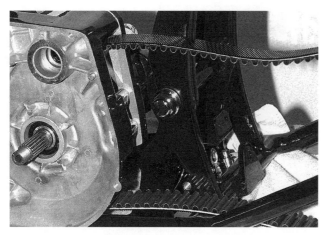

On this Donnie-Smith designed frame the support plates are moved in, which makes for plenty of belt-to-frame clearance even with extra wide tires installed.

A BDL belt drive is used for the primary, in lieu of the standard chain. The clutch assembly is part of the BDL assembly.

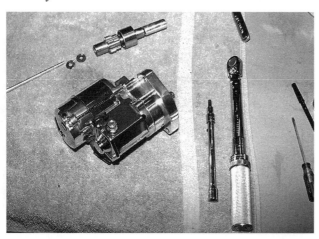

The starter used to turn over the big V-twin is from Spyke. Note the torque wrench, used to tighten most of the nuts and bolts on this hand-built special.

The belt used here is a 133 tooth belt, the recommended belt for this frame when combined with a standard 32 tooth drive and 70 tooth driven pulley. As Donnie explains, "The more typical set up for these two pulleys is a 132 tooth belt. But we wanted to move the rear wheel back just a little in the frame, and the longer belt allowed us to do that."

Next comes the swingarm installation, which is more easily done with a second set of hands. Donnie holds the swingarm in place while John puts the chrome and hardened pivot bolts in place with a star washer under the head of each one.

With the inner primary bolted on for the last time John can install the belt-style primary drive from BDL. "I like the belt drive primary for a number of reasons," explains Donnie. "It's quieter, it can't leak and it's just less messy. But maybe the thing I like best about it is that it comes with their own clutch assembly. It's a really good heavy duty clutch, you can put a lot of horsepower through it without any trouble. If we used a regular primary, then we'd have to go out and buy a separate clutch assembly, which ends up being more money in the long run." Once the inner primary is in place John can bolt on the new polished heavy duty starter from Spyke.

Front Fork and Suspension

The triple trees are part of the complete fork assembly from CSI. Part of the trend toward inverted forks, this "upside down" assembly puts the largest diameter part of the fork in the triple trees, which reduces fork flex and unsprung weight at the same time.

After installing the bearing races in the frame's neck the two new triple trees, tapered bearings and stem can be set into place. John uses water resistant wheel bearing grease on the tapered bearings, but doesn't do the final pre-load adjustment until the fork tubes are installed.

The fork tubes slide easily into the triple trees, though in cases where the fit is too tight, the crew at Donnie's use wooden wedges to open up the triple trees just enough that the fork tubes can

The starter is installed to the inner primary before the oil tank is mounted. Note the Donnie Smith special transmission cover.

After the final adjustment of the tapered stem bearings John can install the front wheel with the sixteen inch Avon tire.

The chrome-plated triple trees are part of the CSI inverted fork package. Tapered stem bearings are packed much as you would an automotive wheel bearing.

An extra set of hands helps to keep the rear wheel and caliper bracket lined up while John pushes the axle into place.

Once the trees are in place the fork tubes assemblies can be installed and the pinch bolts tightened.

The rear wheel too is from Hallcraft and measures 16 inches in diameter. Unlike the front this one is five inches across and mounts a 200 series donut from Avon.

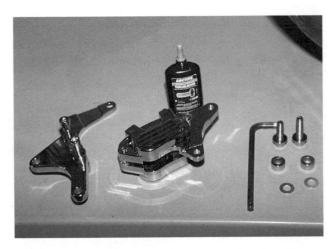

The four piston front calipers use separate brackets. Note the red Loctite and spacers used to correctly position the caliper.

John installs the front caliper brackets next.

Brackets and calipers must be mounted so the caliper will be centered over the rotor.

slide into place. Once the fork tubes are in place John tightens the pinch bolts to 20 foot pounds of torque. And with the complete fork assembly in place the tapered bearings can be adjusted per the instructions in the service manual.

Now John slips the sixteen inch front wheel between the lower fork legs. The wheel is positioned by a spacer used on the right side and the drive for the speedometer on the left.

Though many of the new bikes use electronic speedometers, Donnie chose to use a mechanical drive because of the speedometer. "We wanted to use the small, 1-7/8 inch gauges that CSI offers and mount those in a custom dash. They're nice and small so they fit our plan, they're made in Germany so the quality is pretty good, but the speedometer is mechanical. The cable-drive set up we bought is actually designed for a nineteen inch tire, but the sixteen inch tire (130X16) we used in front has the same outside diameter as a nineteen inch tire, so it works out OK. The drive set up is a two-to-one ratio and that's the same ratio that the speedometer is designed for, so everything works out just fine. If it's off it will only be off just a little. With some of the new electronic speedos you can dial them in so there's no error at all, but none of those come in a small diameter like we wanted."

REAR WHEEL AND ALIGNMENT

Next comes the installation of the rear wheel. John uses the spacers that were cut during the mock-up stage, so the rear wheel pulley will be lined up with the transmission's drive pulley, and the wheel ends up in the center of the frame.

"The thing with custom wheels is, especially with the wide drive frames, no one has a set of spacers," explains Donnie. "You have to individually fit each wheel to the chassis. Normally we start by spacing the pulley over far enough that the belt clears the tire. Then we line the pulley up with the drive pulley on the tranny, then you hope the wheel ends up in the middle of the fender. We try to get the tire in the middle, it doesn't have to be exactly centered, it can be a 1/16 of an inch off.

The center of the fender is lined up with the center of the chassis, so that puts the tire on the frame's centerline as well. In the front, we just cut spacers so the wheel is centered between the fork legs. In this case we had to trim down the speedometer drive a little bit to get the wheel in the center of the fork legs."

In the case of the Founder's bike, the rear tire is the fat 200X16inch tire from Avon, mounted on a five inch Hallcraft rim.

The final installation of the rear wheel requires an extra set of hands and Rob Roehl helps to hold the caliper bracket in place on the right side while John pushes the axle through the bracket and frame slot. Both the front and rear of the bike use chrome-plated GMA four-piston calipers. The rear caliper comes with an integral bracket while the fronts come with their own mounting brackets.

Both the front and rear rotors are from Hallcraft, all are bolted to the hub with grade eight Allen bolts, tightened to 20 foot pounds. John uses blue Loctite in these rotor-to-hub bolts as well as on the pulley-to-hub bolts. On the other side of the wheel is the billet, 70 tooth, rear wheel pulley. These pulley-to-hub bolts are tightened to 65 foot pounds

Once the rear wheel and caliper are installed, John moves to the front of the bike. Each GMA caliper has it's own separate bracket and spacers. John uses the spacers that came with the caliper kits to make sure that each caliper is centered over the polished rotor. Red Loctite is used to ensure the grade eight bolts used to mount the calipers to the mounting brackets don't ever come out. The final tightening of all the caliper mounting bolts is done with a torque wrench set to 40 - 45 foot pounds

The Arlen Ness handle bars with integral risers are mounted next with grips and a throttle assembly from the CSI catalog. The front brakes are controlled by a AMS master cylinder that John mounts on the right side of the bars, while the clutch is operated by a standard cable linkage.

As always, John uses a torque wrench and Loctite on the threads to ensure the bolts are tightened correctly – and stay that way.

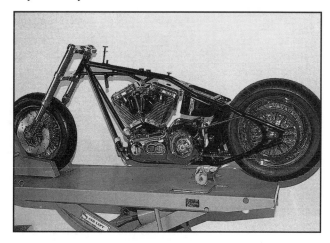

With the starter and both wheels in place it's time to install the oil tank and begin to plumb the frame.

Plumbing incudes the oil lines and the brake lines too. Note the way the speedo cable comes up through the top tube, another detail worked out during the mock-up. Braided lines must be secured so they don't rub the paint.

The built in risers position the bars well back on the bike. Front master cylinder is from AMS, grips and throttle are from the CSI catalog.

It's essential to chase the threads on any parts that have been painted, powder coated or chrome plated – or simply any nut and bolt combination that doesn't screw easily together.

HOSES AND WIRING

The braided brake lines used on this bike are from Goodridge. John routes the two front caliper hoses to a T located under the lower triple tree. From there a single hose runs to the front master cylinder. Matching braided cables are used for the throttle, and also the speedometer. The rear master cylinder and forward controls are from Hurst plumbed to the caliper with another braided brake line.

Installation of the headlight comes next. After chasing the threads on the Allen bolt John installs the headlight to the lower triple tree.

At this point John takes a break so Don Tima can build and install the one-off wiring harness. As Tima explains, "Buying a complete factory harness and then cutting it all up to fit our bike is cost prohibitive. We just make our own harness using stock colors. That way I can make it long enough to fit the stretched frame. And we use the pre-1994 Harley-Davidson plugs and factory wiring colors throughout, so it's easy for any trained mechanic to diagnose if there's a problem. Whether you should have a harness built from scratch or use a factory-style harness depends on the application."

In 1994 Harley went to

The sheet metal goes on last. Front and rear fenders are from Jesse James. The gas tanks started life as four-gallon Fat Bob tanks from CSI before being extended by Rob Roehl.

the water-proof type of connectors, which Tima calls "far superior." Despite their superiority, a number of builders continue to use the earlier style harnesses and components.

The custom Don-Tima harness is easier to hide inside the frame than a full factory harness would be. With no blinkers and the headlight and ignition switches placed on the Donnie Smith coil bracket, the simplified harness works just fine. "I put a connector behind the coils," explains Don. "That way, when it's time to service the engine or remove the coils for any reason, you can just unbolt the bracket and unplug the harness right behind the coil bracket." The coils themselves are from Dyna, controlled by a Crane HI-4 ignition system.

"I use a thirty amp breaker right off the main battery feed, and then one more, fifteen amp breaker, to protect the light and ignition circuits," explains Don Tima. "This bike has an oil pressure light, which I think is better than a gauge because it's more likely to get your attention, especially at night."

With most of the wiring finished John goes back to the mechanical assembly, starting with the derby cover. Sheet metal comes next. Once again, all these parts have been positioned and massaged to fit during the mock up stage. Both the front and rear fenders are from Jesse James, while the gas tanks were stretched in house by Rob, the resident Tin Man.

The blue paint covering the nice sheet metal is the work of Brian Mahler with subtle graphics, gold leaf and the CSI logo created by Lenni Schwartz.

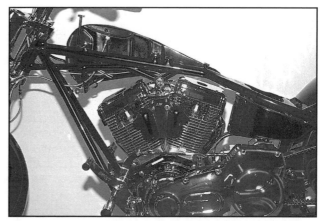

Close up shows the inside of the stretched tank. Standard front mount has been moved and mounts added for the fabricated dash.

Here Rob finishes installation of the tanks. The paint is from Brian Mahler with graphics and CSI logo by Lenni Schwartz.

A Donnie Smith custom minus only the seat and a few details.

The Mock-up

We've stressed the importance of the mock-up before. The need to assemble the whole bike in the raw to ensure that everything fits, both mechanically and aesthetically. Shown here is a mock-up being done at McAllister Motorcycles (part of M-C Specialties). Once finished the bike will be the new ride for Joe Deters of Deters Polishing fame. As a note, this mock-up was completed more recently than the assembly seen in

Chapter 8. As such, this is not only a good example of a mock-up, but of the most recent trends in scratch-built American motorcycles.

THE ASSEMBLY

Mike starts with the bare frame on the hoist and all the major components stacked nearby. Swingarm installation comes next. Mike reminds builders to install the belt before the pivot cross-shaft is bolted in place and to use anti-seize on the pivot bolts.

The next item is the motor, which is a mock-up motor that Mike keeps for just such occasions. Now he can install the transmission, carefully dropping the four studs through the holes in the mounting plate. Flanged nuts are threaded up onto the four studs until they are just snug, and then the engine mounting bolts and nuts are snugged up as well. With the engine and transmission roughly in place the inner primary can be bolted into place, with the 5/8 inch spacer positioned between the engine and the inside of the inner primary.

As was covered in the other two soft-tail assembly sequences in the book, the inner primary is tightened to the engine and transmission before those components are tightened to the frame. Next, Mike installs the oil tank. Some tanks come with the frame, or the frame manufacturer will make a recommendation as to which oil tank best fits their frame. The McAllister frame uses hidden mounts, "I did it that way so you can use any oil tank," explains Mike. "One of my own or one of the standard top-mount tanks."

While installing the Legend air-ride shocks, Mike explains that the unit bolts-in the same as a pair of standard soft-tail shocks, but the alignment is more critical. "You can't force this suspension unit into place, it should bolt in without any binding." The air pump and control unit will be added later.

Before the front fork assembly can be hung on the frame, even for the mock-up, the races for the neck bearings have to be installed. "It's critical that you seat the races all the way," explains Mike, "or the neck bearings keep coming loose. And you have to mask this area off when the frame is painted or powder coated." Mike starts the race into the neck with a soft-faced hammer, then uses the right driver and a ball peen hammer to finish seating the race.

Instead of installing the triple trees followed by the fork tube assemblies, Mike assembles the tubes and the lower tree loosely together, pushes the whole thing into place (the stem up through the

The frame and swingarm are McAllister originals, built in house from DOM mild steel tubing with a wall thickness of .125 inches. The rake angle is 35 degrees.

The frame design uses a spacer on either side between the frame and the swingarm. One shim is thicker than the other, and can thus be used to shift the swingarm slightly side to side

Mike warns that, "at least once, everybody has put in the cross-shaft and then realized they don't have the belt in place yet."

Like most fat-tire frames, this one positions the transmission to the left of the engine centerline which means you need to run a spacer like the one seen here between the engine and the inner primary.

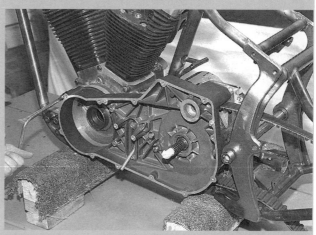

You need an engine, either a real one or a mock-up model, to set in the frame at this point.

It's a good idea to do the complete installation procedure on the inner primary during the mock-up so you know the engine and transmission are correctly aligned.

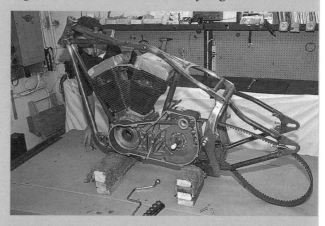

The transmission is the new RevTech 6 speed. This tranny uses an electronic sensor that will communicate with a VDO electronic speedometer. A separate electronic calibration box must be installed when using this transmission with a H-D speedo. Note: the 6-speed gear set will install into a standard 5-speed case.

Though it's not installed yet, Mike will install a belt-style primary from Primo, the Brute 3 with clutch assembly. It's interesting to note that most belt-primaries don't use a compensator sprocket, as the "give" in the belt eliminates the need for the compensator.

The oil tank must be slid into place in just the right way, in order to clear the hidden mount on the frame's center post.

The front fender is designed to match the radius of a 19 inch tire. Though they look cool close to the tire Mike allows room for the tire to grow at speed.

Mike gets ready to install the RMI Legend air suspension unit. Like two miniaturized air-bags from a large semi-truck, this system will provide three inches of ride height adjustment at the touch of a button.

This custom uses a 132 tooth belt stretched between a 32 and a 70 tooth sprocket. Note the tape used to protect the outside of the billet pulley. Most frame manufacturers will recommend a belt and pulley combination.

The front end is from Spyke, though the actual inverted tube assemblies are manufactured by American Suspension and feature speed-sensitive valving and provisions to adjust the ride height.

If the wheel and pulley are positioned correctly the belt will float in the center of the pulley and not crowd over to one side.

neck) then slides the top tree into place over the top of the fork tubes and over the stem, and finally puts the stem nut on to hold it all together.

Installing the front wheel between the fork legs requires two spacers of equal width. Mike explains that most fork manufacturers will provide the spacers if you tell them which wheel you have. The Spyke fork assembly uses an axle that slides through one leg, and screws into a steel sleeve pressed into the bottom of the leg on the other side.

Mike explains the design for the front fender as he sets it in place: "We designed the fender to perfectly match the radius of a nineteen inch tire so we can suck it down really close to the tire. This way it fits right and it looks right too. You have to make sure the wheel is centered in the forks, especially for dual disc brakes. And you need at least 1/2 inch of clearance between the tire and the fender, because the tires will expand that much at speed. And I like to use Nylock nuts on the bolts that mount the fenders so you don't have to worry about them coming loose."

At this point Mike installs the pump for the legends air shocks so he can put some air in the suspension which will simplify rear wheel installation. Mike's procedure for determining the rear wheel and pulley position runs as follows: "With the engine and transmission in the frame, I install the wheel and pulley in the frame with no axle spacers. Then I carefully put light tension on the belt and rotate the wheel in a forward direction so the belt centers itself on the pulley. Then I measure carefully to determine the spacers I need. You have to be sure the belt clears the tire and that the wheel pulley is lined up correctly with the front pulley. When you rotate the wheel in a forward direction the belt should stay in the middle of the pulley and not crowd to one side. You really don't have much choice as to the position of the wheel in the frame, most of that is determined by the position of the transmission and that is determined by the position of the transmission mounting plate(s)."

The rear fender comes next and once it's in place Mike likes to run the suspension through the full range of motion (especially important with the adjustable suspension) to ensure the tire can't rub on the inside of the fender or any fender or seat mounting hardware.

And though Mike doesn't need to wire the bike at this point, it's a good idea to do a rough layout of the wiring during the mock-up stage. If you need to weld on a tab, or drill a hole in a frame tube to run wires through, you definitely want to do that before the paint goes on.

Before ripping the mock-up apart, Mike rolls the bike outside so he can see it "on the street" and make sure all the parts work together to create the look he's after. Sometimes it's hard to really judge the look of a machine that's up on a hoist, six inches in front of your nose.

The strutless rear fender with the unique light assembly is manufactured in-house. During the mock-up it's important to ensure that the tire can't contact the inside of the fender, or any fender/seat mounting bolts or nuts.

The brake caliper is from PM, and comes with the spacers that Mike uses so he can be, "absolutely certain the caliper is centered over the rotor. You also have to be sure the wheel is straight in the frame."

Before the mock-up is finished it's a good idea to roll the bike outside so you can stand back and look it over from various angles.

Chapter Eight

Hands On: A Simple Soft-tail

M-C Specialties builds an OEM-style bike

THE SHOP

Before describing the construction of this bike, it might be helpful to digress and describe the contractor. Mike McAllister became intrigued with the idea of building his own bikes in a full-service shop some eight years ago, shortly after graduating from the M.M.I. mechanic's class in Florida. Scratch building seemed the logical answer to his

This is the finished project ready for the photo shoot- a combination of OEM style frame and hot rod motor, in a *package that's easy on the eyes and not too expensive to build.*

frustration over disassembling and improving existing (sometimes brand new) motorcycles. "It makes more sense to start from scratch," explains Mike. "That way, if what you want is a big-inch motor you don't have to throw away the engine that came with the bike and start over."

Mike opened M-C specialties four years ago and has been building bikes from scratch for three years. Mike's first scratch-built bike was a soft-tail style V-Twin he built for himself. That bike was hardly finished when a customer walked into the shop and asked Mike if he could, "build a nice bike like that for me." M-C Specialties now builds 15 to 20, fairly basic bikes each year. Though he often builds the bikes for a particular customer on a custom-order basis, Mike also builds bikes "on spec." and also sells a variety of kits designed to make it easy for nearly anyone to build their own motorcycle.

When I asked Mike what hints he could pass along to the novice bike builder, he replied that, "You have to be very meticulous. For example, you can't put something part-way together and then plan to tighten the

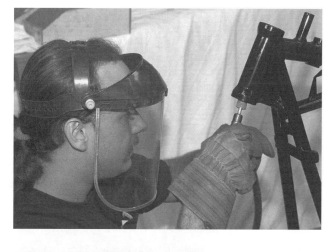

Even with a careful powder coating operator, some of the powder-paint still gets into areas where it isn't wanted. Here Mike cleans paint out of the neck area so the bearing cups will fit correctly.

All the holes must be cleaned up, including the pivot hole for the swingarm assembly.

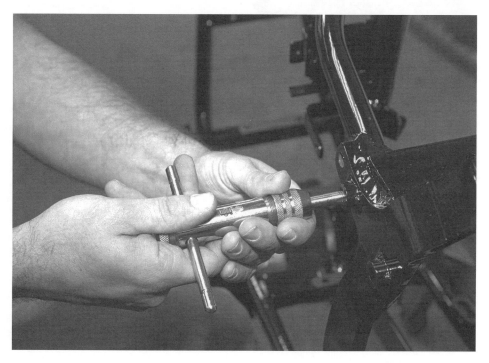

Now is the time to clean up the threads in all the tapped holes. This should be done before you start the assembly no matter what kind of paint is applied, because some of the holes can't be accessed once the parts start going on.

107

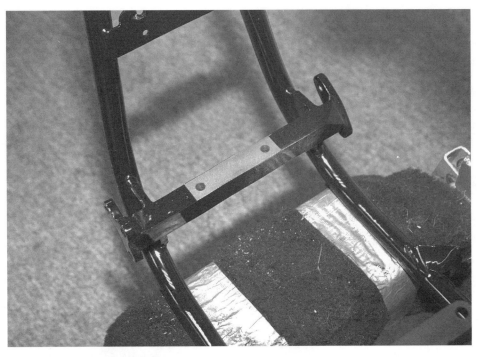

The areas where the motor bolts to the frame were taped so they would remain bare.

bolts later because you'll forget and something will fall off while you're going down the road.

"And it's extremely important to go through the mock-up stage. Sometimes I skip the mock-up stage now because I've built so many bikes with pretty much the same components, but I did it for a long time and for first-time builders it's essential that they assemble the bike 'in the raw' first to be sure everything fits and goes together the way it should. They should also buy a service manual and a parts manual for the bike they're

After the frame is cleaned up Mike starts the assembly by installing the bearing cones for the neck bearings.

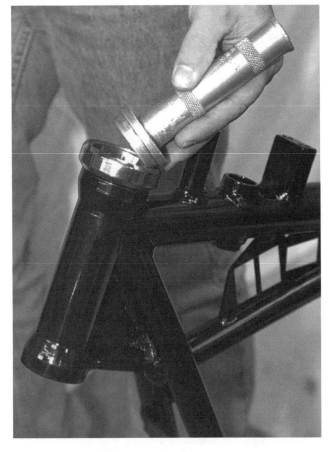

The cones are driven in with a hammer - using the correct bearing driver so there is no damage to the cones.

building, the manuals are really important and will answer lots of questions that come up during construction."

THE COMPONENTS

The bike Mike is starting on is what he calls the basic fatboy-style package. This bike will be based on a Tripoli soft-tail style frame with 30 degrees of rake and no stretch. The Tripoli frame is almost an inch taller than a factory frame which means it will easily accommodate a taller, stroker motor. The extra height also leaves more room on top of the motor so you can see the motor more easily and also gives plenty of room to get in there to clean.

A small hydraulic jack is used here to spread the back of the frame slightly and make it easier to slide the swingarm into place.

For motive power this bike will carry a hot rod engine of nearly 100 cubic inches. Unlike most large displacement V-Twins, this engine is not a "stroker" but gets its extra cubic inches from an increased bore. Like the rest of the bike, the engine is assembled from parts, starting with S&S super stock cases. Before the assembly started the cases were modified for a large 3-13/16 inch bore (after market cases are much better suited to this type of modification).

The barrels are from Sputhe, filled with Sputhe forged pistons. The combination of stock stroke and oversize pistons yields a total displacement of 97 cubic inches. The heads are stock castings from Harley-Davidson, assembled with thermo cool valve springs from Crane with titanium top collars. The intake valves are stock, paired up with black nitrated, tulip, exhaust valves. Before the installation the heads were milled .050 inch for a boost in compression to about 10 to 1. Operating the valves is an EV 7 camshaft from Andrews with 266 degrees of duration and lift of .560 inch. The bottom end is all stock Harley-

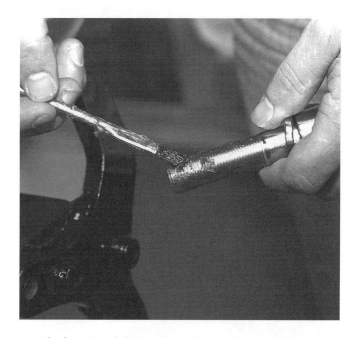

The big pivot bolts are from Garner Wescott, Mike puts heavy grease on the threads so they screw in easily - and will screw back out later if necessary.

Davidson components lubricated by a Harley-Davidson oil pump. Because of the boost in displacement this engine will be equipped with a S&S Super G carburetor.

Behind the big V-Twin Mike will mount a five speed transmission built from a Harley-Davidson Softail transmission case with Andrews gears and main shaft

The primary drive components are all from Harley-Davidson, including the inner and outer primary, the primary chain, compensator sprocket and clutch assembly.

You need plenty of grease on the stem and bearings before installation. The bearings themselves should be packed much as you would a wheel bearing.

After packing the bearings, Mike installs the triple trees.

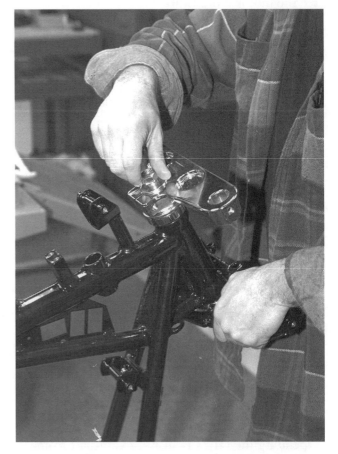

The neck bearings need to be tightened carefully, follow the service manual for the correct procedure.

110

Sturgis cast aluminum wheels measuring 3-1/2 X 16 will hold up both ends. The fork assembly is made up of a Harley-Davidson FLST front end with 41mm tubes and wide glide triple trees. The rear suspension too uses Harley-Davidson components, specifically the factory swingarm, at least partly because Mike thinks they are of higher quality than many of the aftermarket swingarms.

The sheet metal for this bike comes mostly from the factory. Mike likes the Harley-Davidson components for their high quality and reasonable price.

When you consider how many little nuts and bolts there are in a motorcycle, you might wonder how you're going to buy enough hardware to bolt everything together. Fortunately the after market has anticipated your needs with the creation of

The engine in this bike is based on a set of S&S cases and over-size Sputhe barrels. The combination of stock stroke and over-size forged pistons nets 97 cubic inches.

Here Gary sets the second factory head in place. These heads are from H-D, equipped with thermo-cool springs from Crane and black nitrated exhaust valves.

kits. Mike, for example, likes to use a kit for the dash base, "The dash base comes as a kit from Drag Specialties or Custom Chrome (probably other suppliers as well), it makes everything easier and you're not out chasing for all the little parts.

The wiring harness Mike uses for this bike is a Harley-Davidson item designed for 1995 and earlier bikes with the Softail frame. With the Tripoli frame (and many others) the plastic blocks, or harness connectors, snap right into the frame webbing (check the photo to clear up any confusion) for a very neat installation. Note, the harness changed significantly in 1996, so Mike is always sure to buy and use the earlier model harness.

THE ASSEMBLY SEQUENCES

It's time to start the assembly, but before Mike

starts he spends time preparing the frame. Because paint, any paint, won't cover or fill imperfections. Mike explains that if you want your frame to look good you've got to take the time to smooth off the lumps and bumps left there by the factory. Even if you don't want to "mold" the frame, it makes good sense, especially in a situation where the frame is already bare, to take the time to make it look as good as possible before beginning paint

Gary tightens the head bolts in three steps, following the factory sequence and specifications.

and assembly.

Because Mike is intimately familiar with these frames he knows exactly where they need the most attention. "The back of the frame, the big plates that make up the rear of the soft-tail style frame, those parts are flame cut and they're kind of rough," explains Mike. "So I always spend some time sanding and grinding those areas.

Mike starts by taking off the shipping labels with a razor blade and lacquer thinner. Next he enlarges the hole for the fork lock so a larger padlock can be used. Then he starts at the rear of the frame, on the back of the big side plates, working with an angle die-grinder and a 60 grit grinding pad. Mike works to smooth off the rough texture left by the manufacturing process. The small grinder and pad make it easier to get into the crevices and inside of curves that would be hard to reach with a larger tool.

After smoothing out the worst of the peaks and valleys, Mike finishes everything with a 3M Scotch-Brite pad. In addition to the back side plates, Mike goes over any rough areas he finds, eliminating nicks that might occur during shipping, for example. He warns other builders to

Gary is a meticulous builder and likes to lay everything out ahead of time - This way it's easier to find the right part and obvious if something is missing.

avoid grinding on the welds, "because they're what holds the bike together." If the welds are really ugly, then go all the way and mold the frame with plastic filler. In the case of Mike's frame, after cleaning up all the rough edges, it goes out for powder coating, a process that is covered in a Side-Bar in Chapter 2.

THE FINISHED FRAME

Before beginning the assembly Mike cuts out the shipping spreader between the fender struts and runs a tap into all the holes in the frame. He does this whether or not the frame was powder coated, explaining "Sometimes a hole is mis-taped at the factory or bumped and damaged in shipping. The point is, it's easier to find and repair now than when the bike is partly assembled. Some of the holes, like those for the coil cover, are inac-

Gary marks each shaft so he can count the number of rotations during the adjusting process.

Each pushrod is a different length and must be installed in the correct location.

cessible and cannot be tapped once the engine and transmission are in place."

Mike explains that it's also important to sand the inside of the neck where the bearing cones for the fork mount. That way the I.D. of the neck is the correct dimension and the cones press in correctly. It's also important to clean up the hole in the big side plates where the swing arm pivots.

Next, Mike drives the bearing races (or cones) into the neck. It's important to use the right driver, one that matches the inside shape of the race, so as not to damage the bearing race. Note: When the fork assembly is mounted to the bike Mike will set up the tapered bearings according to the procedure in the factory service manual - and check the adjustment after 500 miles.

113

After the valves are adjusted Gary can finish the top end assembly

INSTALLATION OF THE SWINGARM

The swing-axis tube is from H-D and comes powder coated. Mike warns builders to make sure the bolts screw in before you start. It's a good idea to put some grease on the threads of the bolts. The big "Allen" pivot bolts he uses are from Gardner Wescott, Mike likes them because they're more attractive than the factory bolts. These large bolts are torqued to 150 foot pounds. Mike likes to, "finish each step and not leave it half done - that way you don't forget that you were going to tighten that bolt later."

FINAL MOTOR ASSEMBLY AND INSTALLATION

Gary Grimes, from Minneapolis is the man in charge of the motor assembly. Rather than cover the entire assembly, we pick up as Gary gets ready

to install the cylinder heads.

Gary uses a copper O-ring type of head gasket and a Viton O ring for the oil return galley. The heads are set in place and torqued down in three steps, following the sequence outlined in the service manual, Gary first tightens each bolt to seven to nine foot pounds, then to 12 to 14 foot pounds. The final step is to turn each bolt an additional quarter turn. (Note, the specific torque recommendations may vary with certain after market gaskets and engines.)

Before installing the rocker box assemblies, Gary drops in the adjustable Andrews push rods. The push rods are not all the same length and Gary uses the longest one for the front exhaust valve, the next longest on the rear exhaust, then the other two in the center.

Then it's time to install the rocker assemblies

"Clothes pins" are used to hold the pushrod tubes up out of the way so Gary can adjust each valve - 4 to 5 turns past zero lash.

and boxes. Gary puts a little Gasgacinch sealer on the rocker box (base) gaskets before he installs the rocker box and arm assemblies.

To adjust the valves Gary first rotates the engine to find the lowest point on the cam, then adjusts that pushrod to zero lash. Now he marks the pushrod and then lengthens it 4 to 5 complete revolutions.

At this point Mike is ready to install the transmission. This is a pretty straightforward endeavor, except for just a few tricks.

Like remembering to install the transmission with

Rubber bands are used to hold the rear motor mount bolts in place but up out of the way during the installation.

Watch the mounting pads, they may be slightly out of align. Engine and tranny must sit square on mounts.

The five speed transmission is made up of a factory case equipped with Andrews gears.

the bolts facing up, because if they face down they run into the shocks. As mentioned in the powder coating section in Chapter 2, it's important that the pads the transmission and engine mount to be free of paint. Mike uses an installation kit from Gardner Wescott with chrome plated motor mount bolts.

Once the transmission is sitting loosely in the frame it's time to set in the engine. But first Mike positions the back motor mount bolts

Mike bolts the inner primary loosely in place before the engine and transmission mounting bolts are tightened.

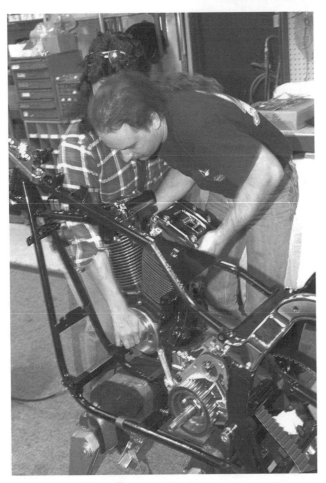

These things aren't light, so get a friend to help, and set the bottom end in first.

into the engine cases, held up with rubber bands (check the photo so this will make more sense). Mike and Gary set the motor in from the right side, and they set the bottom end in first and then tip in the top. Next they drop in the motor mount bolts and make sure the motor is sitting square on the mounts. During the mock-up stage it's important to make sure both engine and transmission sit square on their mounting pads (sometimes the mounts are not square and need to be shimmed).

At this point the motor and transmission are both sitting loose in the frame. The next step is the installation of the inner primary. In order to ensure that the entire driveline is installed correctly and that the engine and transmission mounting points on the frame are correctly located, it is important to follow a specific sequence. Briefly, it goes like this:

1. Get the engine and transmission sitting loose in the frame.

2. Loosely bolt the inner primary to the engine and transmission.

3. Tighten inner-primary to engine bolts first.

4. Tighten inner-primary to transmission bolts.

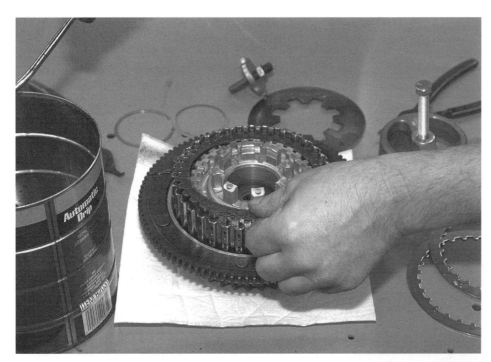

The fiber discs are soaked in primary lube overnight before being installed on the clutch hub.

another. And watch the surface between the inner primary and the engine, you can check it with a feeler gauge, there shouldn't be any gaps there.

Mike likes to wait with the final installation of the inner primary until the front bolts for the shocks are installed. Once the shocks are installed (with locktite on the threads) then the inner primary is installed for the last time.

CLUTCH AND DRIVELINE

5. Get down on your hands and knees and see if the engine and transmission seem to be sitting square on the mounting pads. If so, tighten the engine to frame bolts. Now tighten the transmission mounting bolts: the four transmission-to-frame mounting bolts, two on each end, and then the five big flanged nuts.

After going through this procedure, you might think you're through mounting the engine and transmission, but really the fun has just begun.

To ensure that the engine and transmission are lined up correctly in relation to each other, you need to take off the inner primary and then see if it will slide back on with no hassle. If it won't go back on, the engine and transmission are not aligned. Any attempt to force the parts together will usually break the inner primary.

When Mike encounters a problem like this he shims the transmission until the inner primary will go on and off with no trouble. Mike cautions builders to watch the front transmission mount, just behind the down-tube. "If the jig that the frame manufacturer used is worn a little bit, then the various mounting points aren't all true to one

This tool is used to compress the clutch pack so the retaining ring can be installed.

Once the clutch pack is complete the primary drive is put together.

Next, the complete primary assembly is set in place.

Before assembling the new clutch assembly, Mike soaks the fiber clutch discs in primary lube overnight. That way you get good clutch action and clean shifts right away.

The drive line assembly is all factory parts. The clutch assembly is assembled per the factory manual, which involves compressing the clutch pack with a special tool so the retaining ring can be installed. Next, Mike and Gary assemble the front sprocket, chain, adjuster and clutch assembly into one larger "assembly" and slide it into place. Note the main shaft nut which holds the clutch assembly in place is a left-hand thread.

Both the main shaft nut and the nut for the compensator sprocket (the front drive sprocket) should be tightened with a torque wrench to factory specifications. The specification for the primary chain tension is 5/8 to 7/8 inches of flex cold, Mike sets the primary chain up on the tight side of the specification because all the parts are new. Finally it's time to install the outer primary and fill it with lube.

After packing the neck bearings Mike installs the wide-glide triple trees and tightens the top nut to factory specs. Next it's a matter of sliding the assembled fork tubes into place. Mike notes that you should be sure

The manual gives a range for the primary chain adjustment (controlled by the adjusting pad near the bottom of the case). Mike likes to set the tension on the tight side of the range because the parts are new and likely to stretch.

there's room for a finger between the trees, bars and assorted hardware - and the tank itself, so you don't put a big ding in the tank the first time you go lock to lock in the parking lot.

WIRING

Most bike builders use a factory harness as the basis for the wiring on their scratch-built machines. Mike is no different and uses a 1995 and earlier Softail harness for this particular bike. Even with the factory harness there remains plenty of "hand work." This is a case where if you're not good with wiring the best thing to do is turn the job over to an experienced mechanic.

M-C specialties makes up their own mini harnesses, one for the dash and another for the tail light. The harness for each side of the bars (for the starter, horn switch and so on) come with the switch assemblies. Mike adds one extra wire to the harness for each side so the customer can add "whiskers" turn signal lights. He warns that not all the switch harnesses are the same. Some are longer than others which makes them easy to use if the bars are fairly tall.

To wire the dash, Mike works off of a schematic that he took from a manu-

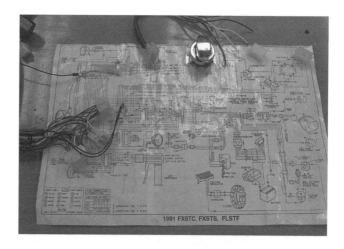

Wiring this bike is made easier by the wiring diagram Mike had blown up and laminated.

These blocks at the front of the Softail harness snap into the webbing at the front of the frame.

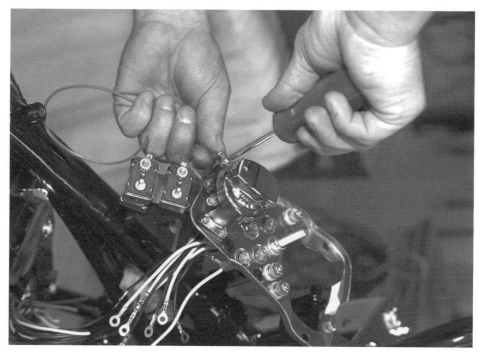

Though some of the wires come already installed in the dash, you (or the person you hire) will have to install wires on the ignition switch and 3 circuit breakers and form those into a small harness.

It's important to route the positive battery cable as shown so it doesn't break later.

You will have to complete the harness for either side of the handle bars, and also the one for the dash. The process starts as you neatly strip the insulation from the wire.

Next you need a package of the small male pins as shown.

al and had enlarged and laminated at the local copy shop. That way he doesn't need a magnifying glass to decipher all those tiny little lines.

When he makes up the sub-harnesses Mike uses factory wiring colors to ease any future servicing problems. At the front, the factory harness is complete, except for the dash and the two handle bar harnesses. There are three big plugs in the harness that snap into the frame: the back one is for the dash wires, the middle one is for the right side controls and the front one is for the left controls.

For the connector plugs that attach to the three big plugs in the factory harness, Mike buys the plugs in the after market and also buys a box of the small pin connectors which snap into the connector plugs. Each wire in the dash or handle-bar harness must have one of these pin connectors crimped onto the end of the wire, then the connectors must be snapped into the block, obviously in the correct location. Mike readily admits he does plenty of wiring for other people and feels, "Anyone who hasn't wired a bike before shouldn't be afraid to ask for help."

SHEET METAL

Once the wiring is finished, Mike can finish the installation of the sheet metal and lights. At M-C Specialties they often use the factory sheet metal, simply because it needs less body work before the paint is applied. Mike uses Nylock nuts for much of the sheet metal to avoid any chance the bolts will come loose.

The rear fender is attached with grade-eight button-head bolts. Mike leaves the struts loose until all the bolts are loosely attached. He also uses some thin backing material between the struts and the fender to avoid scratching up the nice paint on the fender as it's installed.

With the fender mounted to the bike, the next task is to mount the tail light and then the license plate mount. Next comes the dash cover and the tanks, all of which needs to be done in concert.

For the fat-bob style tanks Mike likes to leave the two front mount assemblies loose on the frame, then mount the tank. He puts bolts in the two front mounts first, then drops a bolt into the rear hole.

When he sets the dash cover on, Mike checks that the speedometer is at the right height and the ignition switch is in the middle of the opening so it will turn easily.

Slip the wire into the pin connector. Each connector has a barb which holds it into the terminal block.

Then use the correct crimping tool to crimp the pin connector onto both the wire and the insulation - if you do a bad job or use a pliers to do the crimping the pin won't slide into the terminal block.

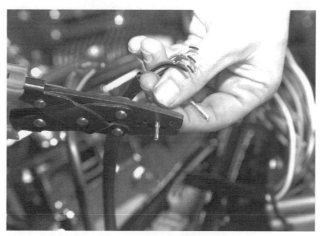

After the connector pins are slipped into the correct location in the terminal block - according to the wiring diagram - each block is plugged into the matching block in the factory wiring harness.

The sheet metal on this bike is from Harley-Davidson, with an electric blue paint job by Jerry Snyder at M-C Specialties.

Mike uses self-locking ny-lock nuts on the back side of the Allen bolts that hold on the front fender.

INSTALL THE REAR WHEEL

There is no wide-drive kit used on this bike, so installation of the wheel is pretty straightforward. The engine and transmission are already installed in the location dictated by the mounting pads on the frame. The trick is to correctly mount the wheel and rear brake caliper.

Because this bike carries a stock width tire on a Sturgis wheel (which in this case mounts the wheel and drive sprocket in the factory location) all Mike has to do is use the factory axle and left side spacer between the driven sprocket and the frame. The bracket used to mount the caliper on the right side is the same width as the factory bracket, helping to keep this a simple installation.

Mike explains that, "Basically, you set the wheel up in what you think is the right location, adjust the belt tension, set up the caliper, tighten the axle nut and then see how the belt looks (more on the belt to come). Lots of people mount the caliper wrong. You have to use spacers to move the caliper bracket or even the rotor so the caliper is centered over the rotor. You want the pistons on either side of the caliper to travel

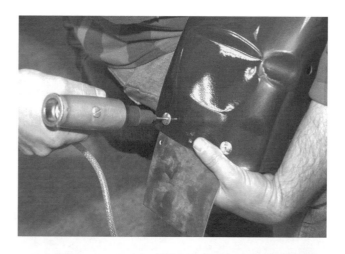

The small mud flap at the front of the rear fender is installed with pop-rivets.

By using some scrap paper between the fender and rail, Mike avoids scratching the fender during the installation.

Here we see Mike's project with the sheet metal installed, waiting for the wheels.

Because this is an OEM style frame without a wide-drive kit, Mike will use a factory axle and spacers to correctly position the wheel and pulley in the swingarm.

exactly the same distance when the brakes are applied.

Mike uses the simple little gauge, as shown, to check that the position of the axle is the same from side to side. Most manuals have a diagram so you can make a similar measuring tool.

Checking that the belt is centered and running true is largely a visual matter. With the wheel in place and the axle nut tightened, Mike rotates the tire in the direction of travel and makes sure the belt isn't crowding up against one side of the wheel pulley. He spends

The speedo head should be flush with the dash cover and centered. The ignition switch should turn easily.

This two-piston caliper is centered over the rotor - so each piston moves the same amount on application.

some time eye-balling the belt from just behind the bike. If the belt is off very much you can usually spot it from this angle.

The drive belt is adjusted to factory specification for tension with the bike on the ground (preferably with a rider aboard). The tension and position of the belt should be checked after 10 to 50 miles - be sure the belt hasn't stretched and that it isn't wearing on one side of the pulley.

When it's all done, Mike has a simple soft-tail, with trick paint and a nice strong motor.

Here Mike hold the wheel up and gets the belt set in place.

This is the simple tool used to correctly position the wheel in the swingarm as the belt tension is adjusted (most service manuals show you how to make these tools).

Chapter Nine

Hands On: A Pro-Street Project

Minneapolis Custom builds one to run hard

THE SHOP

Minneapolis Custom Cycle has been building scratch-built bikes for five years now. Though soft-tail style bikes are always popular, Minneapolis Custom Cycles builds more rubber-mounts than anything else. Perhaps because Pat Matter, the shop's owner, believes in building bikes that run and run hard. "I will build a customer a soft-tail style bike, but I think a rubber-mount makes a better bike. There's less vibration and they handle

Pat Matter from Minneapolis Custom Cycles and one of the nearly 60 motorcycles they create each year.

better."

Because they have a full machine shop, assembly area and chassis dyno, Pat's shop is well equipped to turn out nearly 60 bikes per year. Most of those have to be classified as high performance V-Twins. "We go through a specification sheet with the customer," explains Pat. "We can build whatever that new owner wants with any engine they desire. But a lot of people go for what I call our 'Stage 1' engine. We start with Delkron cases, add Harley-Davidson flywheels, Wiseco three and a half inch pistons (same as stock), one of Carl's 575 camshafts, factory heads that we port, and a Series E carburetor from S&S. These engines make about 90 horses at the rear wheel with only eighty cubic inches and it isn't a real expensive package."

Most of the rubber-mount bikes to come out of the Minneapolis Custom shop are based on the Kenny Boyce Pro Street frame with the offset swingarm and motor mount so a 160 or larger rear tire can be used in the rear. Typical front forks are mid or wide-glide assemblies, based on new Harley-Davidson 41mm tubes and stock triple trees. The most common wiring harness is a Softail unit, unless the frame is one of the Tripoli FXR-clones.

Pat's reports that, "We like to stick with things we know work. Our bikes are

The start of the project is this Kenny Boyce Pro Street frame.

Richard installs the widened FXR fender. The Kenny Boyce frame has threaded mounting points, so the fender bolts on from the inside with button-head bolts while the fender rails bolt on from the outside.

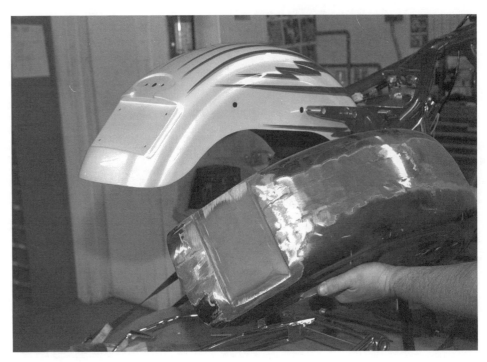

Here's one of their modified and widened fenders in the raw. Note how they create a recess for the license plate and sometimes the cat's eye taillight.

serviceable. That's why we use plenty of H-D components and commonly available parts. The exotic stuff is harder to service. When you build a bike for someone, you have to ask yourself, 'what if it breaks down on the way to Sturgis, will the owner be able to get it repaired?'"

THE COMPONENTS

The frame for the bike in question is a Kenny Boyce Pro Street frame with the offset kit for a wide rear tire, and no extra stretch or rake. This kit offsets the engine and tranny as a unit and then uses a wider

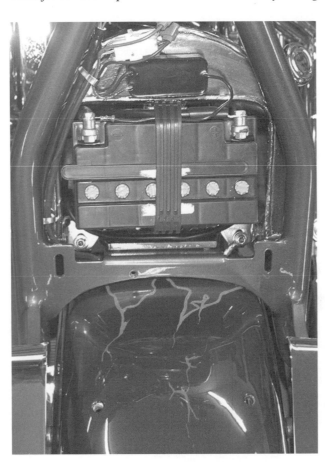

One of the things to check during the mock-up stage: Does the fender match the shape of the frame brace.

When in doubt, use plenty of Loctite, on the fender rails and nearly anything else.

This is the oil tank that comes with the KB frame, supported by a bracket that hangs off the top tube, though other tanks could be adapted as well.

ASSEMBLY SEQUENCE
CHASSIS

This bike is assembled by Richard Rohda, one of the mechanic's at Minneapolis Custom Cycle. Richard likes to have 6-1/2 to 7 inches of clearance between bottom of frame tube and the ground. As a rule of thumb, the center of the front axle should line up with the bottom frame tube when the bike is sitting on the hoist.

Richard uses 41mm

swingarm to accommodate the wider tire and belt drive. The swingarm is a widened FXR unit built in-house and then sent out for chrome plating.

As mentioned, the harness is designed for a Softail, though a few components will be moved, meaning the harness will have to be modified slightly. Also used is a factory self-canceling module for the turn signals, which

> **…you have to ask yourself, 'what if it breaks down on the way to Sturgis, will the owner be able to get it repaired?'"**

must be used in conjunction with a Badlands unit to make sure the unit will work correctly with the non-stock turn signals.

The Kenny Boyce frames have mounting points designed to work with FXR fenders. As the frame is wider than a stock frame, the stock fender is too narrow. At Minneapolis Custom they widen a FXR fender and use that with the Pro Street frame.

Wide-glide triple tree work on the KB frame just fine after a little modification of the lower tree.

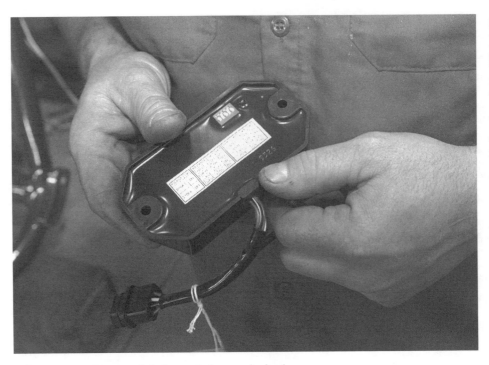

The Dyna ignition module has switches on the back so you can set different curves and rev limits. The module must be mounted so you can see the light in corner.

Here's the dash base and upper tank-mounting bracket sitting loosely on the frame. Wiring harness is a factory Softail unit.

fork legs designed for a FXST (these are left at stock length) and mounts them in factory Softail triple trees. The fork stop in the lower tree will work with the tab on the neck of the Kenny Boyce frame. As mentioned earlier, the back of the lower triple tree was trimmed away to do this.

WIRING

This frame is set up for fat-bob style tanks, and the Softail harness works best. Richard notes that sometimes he runs the wiring up inside the top tube, though it's extra work. There is a hole at the back of the top tube, but running the wires inside the top tube means drilling a hole up near the neck and sometimes another where the upper engine mount is.

For this bike the wires will not run inside the frame and one of the first things Richard does is to drill two holes in the bottom cross member for the ignition module. The Dyna 2000 ignition module must first have the small pins set in the right position: to determine the rev limit, the advance and whether it will be used in single or double-fire mode. The light on back of the module is used to set the static timing, so the module is mounted so you can see the light if you look down under the frame. Richard notes that the only trouble they've had with these modules is when someone used solid copper plug wires instead of the recommended carbon core plug wires.

With the module mounted in the new position, the two wires that run from the module to the coil are too short. Richard lengthens the pink and white wires (pink is control or trigger, white is the power - be sure your harness uses the same color code) with wires of the same color and gauge, and runs those up through the factory harness to the middle of the top tube, near the motor mount, to where the coil will mount.

Each wire connection is soldered and then sealed with shrink tubes. When he's all done, the work is so neat it's hard to tell the harness didn't come this way. He also cuts and eliminates the wire for the factory vacuum switch, as it is not used with this ignition module. Richard follows the same basic procedure to extend the wires for the horn, which will be moved from the stock location.

The dash base is a stock Harley-Davidson part. Most of the necessary wires for the dash harness are already included as part of the dash base assembly. Additional wires for the three circuit breakers will have to be run when the dash base harness is finished. Richard

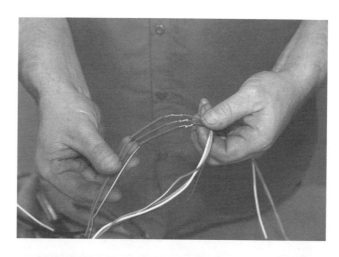

With the module mounted on the lower cross-brace the wires to the coil are too short and must be lengthened.

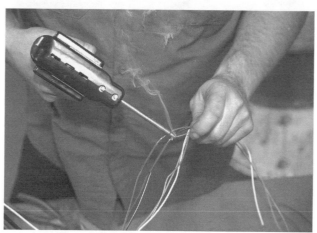

Using wires that match the size and color of the factory wires, Richard carefully solders each connection.

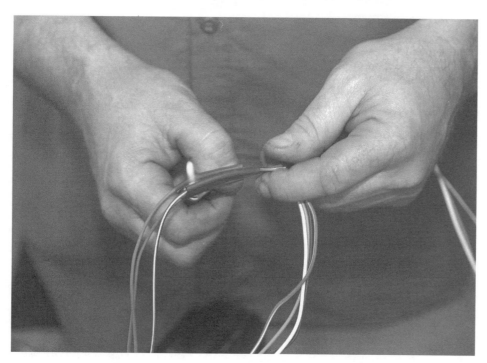

Next the shrink tubes are slid over each soldered joint and warmed up so they shrink and waterproof each connection.

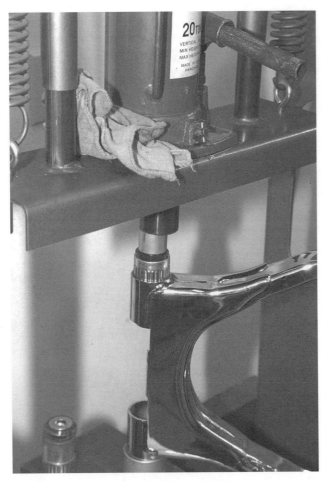

A hydraulic press is used to install new bushings in the modified FXR swingarm.

The rear fender is installed with chrome Allen head bolts on the outside and chrome button-head bolts inside. Of note. the mounting bungs on the back of the Kenny Boyce frame are not just holes, but are threaded on the inside. This way the button head bolts can be screwed in from the inside leaving no bolt head or nut on the inside of the fender to catch on the tire. As noted earlier, a tube has already been welded up into the corner of the fender and the wires for the taillight will be run through that tube.

Richard installs the gas tanks, while the upper, front mounting assembly is still loose. This upper mounting point is slotted so it can give a little. He uses rubber-mounted tanks, explaining that, "No one uses the solid mount tanks anymore."

OFFSET KIT AND SWINGARM

The Kenny Boyce Offset Kit works by moving

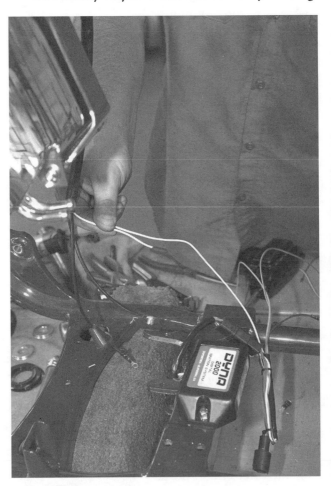

Here you can see how the module was mounted to the lower frame brace.

explains that, "The three circuit breakers that mount to the dash base are 15 amp breakers. The main breaker is 30 amps and I will mount it in back near the battery in a location that you can get at without taking anything apart. Power comes from the battery to main breaker, then up to the ignition switch, through the brown wire in the harness. This wire comes into the rear-most of the three wiring blocks located under the top tube. From there power goes to the ignition switch, then out to the three smaller, 15 amp breakers and to the various circuits."

BODY PARTS

The rear fender is a FXR unit that the boys at Minneapolis Custom widen in-house and then have painted. An area at the back of the fender is recessed for an Arlen Ness cat's-eye taillight and billet license plate holder with turn signals.

With an adapted valve-seat grinding tool Richard removed 3/8 of an inch from the left side of the transmission mount (any small grinder could be used for this, though the valve-seat tool is a neat way to do it).

like grease might."

After the pivot shaft is in place, the outer endcaps are bolted on. You have to make sure the small pins on each endcap slide into the recesses in the outer bushings so everything is positioned correctly. Richard is careful to use loctite on the end-cap bolts and the pivot shaft nut, explaining, "You've got to loctite the shit out of the pivot shaft nut or it's guaranteed to come loose." When he's all through the swingarm

the engine and transmission over to the left. Typically this is accomplished by taking .375 inches of material off the left side of the rear mount for the FXR-style transmission case, and compensating for the lost material by using a spacer of the same dimension on the right side of the rear transmission mount.

Richard uses an adapted valve seat tool to neatly take off the material on the left side of the mount. Then the transmission is set up loosely in the frame, the spacer is held in place on the right side and the pivot shaft is slid through the outer pivot bushings, the swingarm and the rear transmission mount. Before sliding the pivot shaft through, Richard lubricates it with anti-seize, explaining that, "the anti-seize will never work out of there

> **Richard is careful to use locktite on the end-cap bolts and the pivot shaft nut...**

Here you can see how the removal of material on the left side of the transmission mount allows the transmission to slide over in the swingarm.

133

With the transmission sitting loosely in the frame, Richard slides the pivot shaft into place.

This close-up shows the spacer that's used on the right side of the transmission and the new outer bushing.

Next comes installation of the swingarm end caps.

moves up and down easily.

For rear shock absorbers, Richard usually uses 13 inch shocks, substituting 12 inch units if the customer wants the bike just a bit lower.

Note, deadlines being what they are, I was not able to follow this bike through to completion. I did ask Richard how he aligned the engine and transmission, which is a much different procedure for this rubber-mount frame than for a solid mount frame. He outlined the procedure as follows:

First, make sure the rear wheel pulley lines up with the pulley for transmission. This is primarily a matter of positioning the wheel correctly in the swingarm.

Once the two pulleys are aligned, you still have to align the whole drivetrain relative to the two wheels. The procedures breaks down into three steps.

1. Put a level on the front brake rotor, move the bike so the rotor is perfectly vertical. Now check to see if the rear brake rotor is level. If not adjust the top heim joint until it is.

2. Make sure the drive belt tension is correctly adjusted and that the wheel is centered in the swingarm, according to the procedure in the service manual. For his reference point, Richard uses center of the swingarm pivot, not the small hole in the side of the later model

swingarm.

3. Use two long straight edges to align the two wheels so they run straight together. If they don't, adjust the rear wheel position with the front heim joint.

Richard's final words of advice regards the importance of a mock-up, "We still do a mock-up on some of our bikes, and we build more bikes than almost any other shop. Some of those holes that are supposed to line up don't, so you have to check it before everything gets painted."

Deadliness are hell. This is the "finished" twin-shock bike from Minneapolis Custom, with wiring mostly installed and some great looking sheet metal.

With Loctite on the threads, Richard bolts in the end caps and chrome covers.

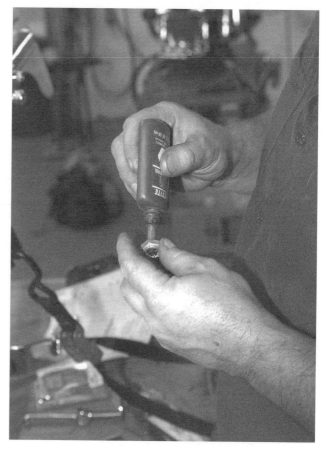

Put plenty of Loctite on the shaft nut before installation and check all the nuts and bolts after 500 miles.

Chapter Ten

A Compendium of Projects

A variety of bikes in the mock-up stage

AN ARLEN NESS CONVERTIBLE

The series of bikes seen here are what Arlen calls his new "convertibles." Avid motorcycle enthusiasts seem to be building different bikes for different occasions, one for bar hopping and one for long distance rides.

Arlen though it might be nice if you could simply make one bike perform more than one duty, that way you would only need one bike in the garage. The bikes seen under construction here are designed from the start to work as both a long distance touring rig and a

In fully dressed form, these new convertibles make a great road bike with fairing, floor boards and taildragger fend- *ers. To "convert" the bike to bar-hopping mode, just take off the fairing and install the second set of fenders.*

stripped down in-town ride. The assembly pictures were taken in the Arlen Ness shop by Carmina Besson, the woman responsible for the beautiful Arlen Ness catalog. All bikes are based on the new rubber-mount frame built from large diameter chrome-moly tubing, with a five inch stretch and a 38 degree fork angle. The engines in these versatile V-Twins is a 80 cubic inch mill with polished cases, painted and polished cylinders and ported heads. The camshaft is from Crane while the carburetor is from S&S. Each bike carries the full range of Arlen's billet engine parts, including rocker boxes, lifter blocks, cam cover and air cleaner. Eighteen inch spoked, Akront rims with Ness hubs are used at either end and help give the bikes a classic appearance. For stopping power these bikes rely on Arlen's billet calipers and polished rotors. House of Kolor paint applied by Bryan Kinney gives the bikes their bright hues with accents by Carl Brouhard. Before assuming that expensive bikes like these never see any road miles, consider that a group of these bikes was seen in Sturgis this year, and all were ridden there from Arlen's shop in San Leandro, California.

Arlen's new convertible bikes start life as a bare frame, in this case one of the new 1-1/4 inch diameter models with a full five inches of stretch and a 38 degree fork angle.

Partly finished, you can better see the Arlen Ness primary, the dual-rail swingarm and the pair of 18 inch Akront rims laced to Arlen Ness hubs.

Here you can see one of the bikes nearly finished. Note how the rear axle mounting point is moved to the top of the swingarm to lower the bike. Engine is an 80 cubic inch unit built in the Arlen Ness shop with factory flywheels, STD pistons, polished aftermarket cases, ported factory heads, a Crane cam and Bub pipes.

The gas tank on this mock-up in Donnie Smith's shop is an aftermarket quick-bob tank, extended by Rob Roehl, the same man who fabricated the custom dash.

The frame on this bike is from Kenny Boyce and will carry a fat rear tire with the help of an offset transmission and offset engine mounts.

ALWAYS BUSY, DONNIE SMITH

Though Donnie Smith's shop may not be massive, there's no shortage of work going in and out the door. Every time I stop by (often a weekly event) there's a new bike being mocked-up on the hoist with another waiting in the corner and one more being assembled in the other room.

Presented here are two of the bikes seen recently in Donnie's shop, while a third bike is presented at the end of this chapter (Jon Kosmoski's bike). The first bike is built around a Kenny Boyce frame with the wide-drive kit. Like most of these bikes the transmission is an FXR-style five speed with the modified rear mount to shift the drivetrain over to the left.

The gas tank on this bike started out as an aftermarket tank before Rob Roehl, Donnie's Number One Man, got his hands on it. After extending the tank Rob fabricated a dash that runs the length of the tank.

The flipped rear fender was modified too. Rob split it into two pieces and then added a strip of metal down the middle so it would better fit the pro street frame.

Bike number two is similar, in that it uses another Kenny Boyce frame, though that's where the similarity stops. The front end on bike number two is a lovely Ceriani fork assembly with chrome-moly tubes

The 180x17 rear tire requires a fender measuring 8-1/2 inches wide - created by adding a strip of metal to a stock fender.

and machined aluminum "sliders." During the early part of the mock-up session the fork seemed too long, so Donnie did the logical thing, he raked the frame. The new fork angle pushed the front wheel forward and brought the rest of the bike closer to the ground.

The sheet metal on this machine is a little different than most. The tank was a quick-bob style aftermarket tank with two filler caps. Rob Roehl filled the two filler caps and installed a flush mount gas cap (as seen in Chapter Five).

To make the tank better fit the frame Rob also stretched it with a one-piece cap he fabricated and welded in place.

Instead of buying any old catalog seat, Rob bent up a seat base, which will then be sent out to Keith Nybo in New Brighton Minnesota for upholstery.

The fenders are from Jesse James, Boyd Coddington's "motorcycle wheel man." Jesse must crank out the fenders at night when he's not busy trying to keep up with the growing demand for the new Boyds Wheels.

Speaking of wheels, the hoops seen here are not Boyds Wheels, these are PMF wheels. Precision Metal Fabrication is a small company located just south of Minneapolis currently manufacturing a growing line of alloy rims. The rims on this particular bike measure 19 inches in front and 18 in the rear.

Another view shows the Ceriani fork and 19 inch PMF front wheel. Front fender is from Jesse James.

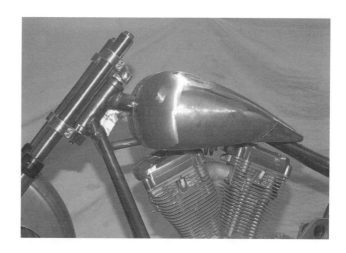

This mock-up shot in Donnie Smith's shop shows the modified quick-bob tank and how the Kenny Boyce frame was raked.

Here you can see the hand-formed seat base, and the 18 inch rear rim from Precision Metal Fabrication.

Steve Laugtug's new bike early in the mock-up stage. The frame is one of Arlen's new rubber-mount designs made from large, inch and a quarter diameter, chrome-moly tubing.

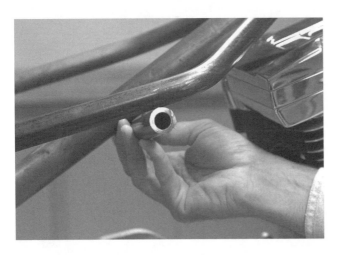

Steve took out a few of the non-essential tubes to clean up the frame, note the heavy wall tubing used in this frame.

STEVE LAUGTUG

Steve Laugtug has owned a number of very high quality bikes and cars. Steve understands first hand that creating a unique machine means spending plenty of time with the fabricators- those men with the ability to craft the parts he needs from raw tubing and sheet steel.

The rewards of building a unique machine are great - when everything goes according to plan. When it doesn't the project can be come a frustrating series of disappointments.

This time Steve decided to make the new bike a relatively simple affair. With all the new aftermarket parts available, Steve decided to build a bolt-together bike.

The frame is one of Arlen's new rubber-mount designs, the fork is from Ceriani and the engine and transmission are straight from Harley-Davidson. Steve chose a new stretched aluminum gas tank and a pair of Jesse's fenders.

It's a good concept, the simple, bolt together bike. But Steve has a keen sense of design so it will be interesting to see if he can live with some of the compromises dictated by the bolt-together concept. Only time will tell.

The sheet metal for Steve's bike is a combination of Jesse James fenders and a hand-formed aluminum gas tank.

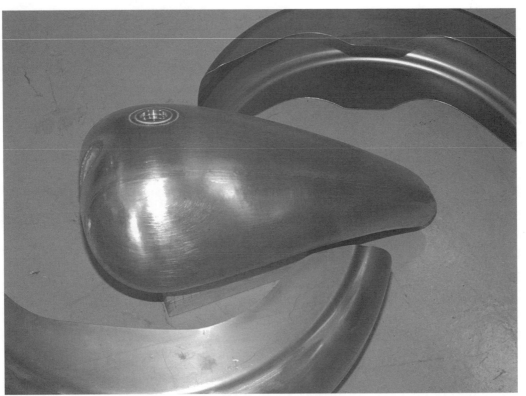

The fork on Steve's new bike is a Ceriani, "upside-down" design. Front rim is from Akront and measures 18x4-1/2 inches.

A frame with a five inch stretch needs a matching aluminum gas tank from Pro One.

One of Steve's goals for this bike is to keep it a simple, bolt-together deal. In keeping with that theme both the 80 cubic inch engine and the FLT transmission are stock units from the local Harley-Davidson dealer.

Not quite ready to ride but already the bike is showing some nice lines. The stretched frame with matching gas tank works well with the Jesse James fenders. Rear Akront rim measures 18x5-3/4 inches. Fender struts will be altered or replaced.

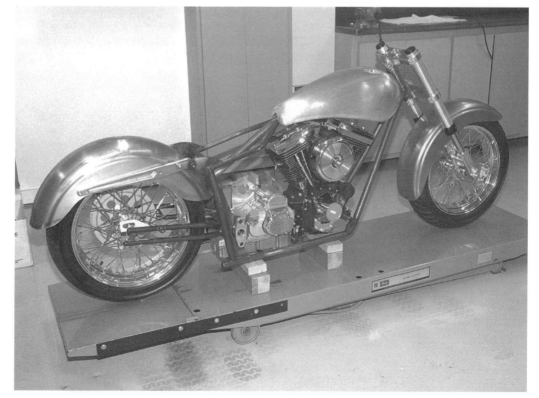

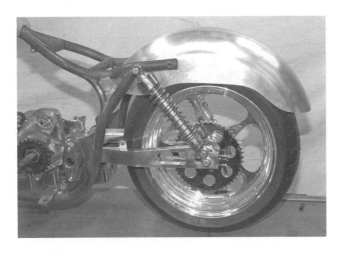

Another Donnie Smith project, this one being built for Jon Kosmoski, owner of the House of Kolor. Note the Boyd billet wheels, trick aluminum fender from Jesse James and massive swingarm.

THE HOUSE OF KOLOR BIKE

Jon Kosmoski, owner of the House of Kolor, likes fast motorcycles. Bikes you can run hard around a corner or up through Spearfish canyon. Jon's bikes have to be more than fast, they have to meet his sense of mechanical precision, each part must measure up to his own high standards.

The bike seen here is another pro-street design, as conceived by Jon Kosmoski. The frame is a high quality twin-shock design from Mark Rowe. For wheels Jon called Boyd Coddington, who sent Jon two beautiful billet wheels that measure 17 inches in back and 19 in front. Jon plans to run a 180-55x17 rear tire like so many builders but will use chain drive instead of the standard belt.

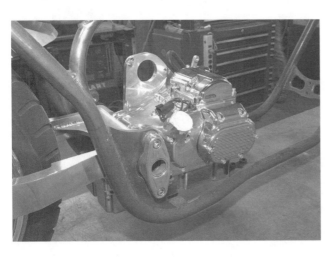

This is a rubber-mount frame equipped with a late model FLT transmission - which puts the oil tank under the transmission and out of the way.

The chain drive may not be the only unusual feature on this bike, because Jon has his own ideas about what makes a great scratch-built motorcycle.

Jon likes to travel first class, thus we have a Mark Rowe frame, Paioli fork and hand-formed aluminum gas tank from Pro One. Donnie thinks that by eliminating the oil tank from it's conventional location he can open up the design of the bike.

DIRECTORY OF SUPPLIERS
FOR YOUR ULTIMATE V-TWIN

Atlas Frames,
16091 Kamana Rd
Apple Valley CA 92307

Arlen Ness Inc
16520 E 14th St.
San Leandro, CA 94578
510 276 3303

Boyds Wheels
Boyds Motorcycle Wheels
10541 Ashdale St
Stanton Cal 90680 714 952 0700

Best Coat Inc
Powder Coating
1557 101st Av N.E.
Blaine, MN 55449
612 785 7086

Custom Chrome,
1 Jacqueline Court
Morgan Hill, CA 95037
408 - 778-0500

Custom Cycle Engineering
1970 Peacock Blvd
Oceanside, CA 92056
619 941 6487

Drag Specialties
9839 W 69th St
Eden Prairie, MN 55344
612 942-7890

Forking by Frank.
945 Ptner Av
Evanston, IL 60202
708 475 1003

Kokesh MC parts
8302 NE Hwy 65
Spring Lake Park, MN 55432
612 786 9050

GMA Engineering
2808 Q street
Omaha, Nebraska, 68107
402 734 6141

House of Kolor
Kustom Paint
2521 27th Av So.
MPLS MN 55406
612 729-1044

Hyperformance
5152A N.E. 12th Av
Pleasant Hill, IA 50317
515 266 6381

Jesse James: Custom Sheet Metal
C/O Boyds Wheels
10541 Ashdale
Stanton CA 90680
714 952 0700

M-C Specialties
1551 101st Av NE
Blaine, MN 55449
612 785 9119

Mid-USA
4937 Fyler
St. Louis MO 63139
314 351 3733
FAX 314 351 6990

Mark Rowe Chassis
148 Batchelder Rd
Seabrook NH 03874
603 474 3330

Morgan's #1 Insurance
2457 Lyndale Av S
Minneapolis MN 55408
612 870 1558

Nempco East
7 Perry Dr.
PO Box 9137
Foxboro MA 02035
508 543 6386

Nybo, Keith,
Upholstery
511 Old Hwy 8
New Brighton MN 55112

O'Phelan Insurance
899 Randolph Av
St. Paul MN 55102
612 228-9663

Performance Machine
15535 Garfield Av
PO Box 1739
Paramount, CA 90723
310 634 6532

Precison Metal Fabrication
Custom Wheels
1646 E Hwy 101
Shakopee, MN 55379
612 496 0053

Pro One
915 W. Foothill Blvd
Azusa CA 91702
818 334 0662

Scherer, Jerry
Custom Paint
11660 347th St
Lindstrom MN 55045

Storz
239 So. Olive St.
Ventura CA 93001
805 641 9540

S&S Cycle
Box 215
Viola, WI 54664
608 627-1497

Sumax
337 Clear Rd.
Oriskany, NY 13424
315 768 1058
315 768 1046 FAX

Tripoli Frames,
Box 45, Site 14, RR #1,
Red Deer Alberta
Canada
403 347 8810

White Brothers
14241 Commerce Drive
Garden Grove, CA 92643
Suspension components
714 692 3404